TOMMI POCKETS

Is there any hope for
a kid like Pockets?

Marsha Hubler

1 Cor 15:10

(Watch for Tommi Pockets
2 + 3!)

ENDORSEMENTS

Marsha Hubler knows well the dreams, angst, longings and disappointments of young people, personified expertly in Tommi Jo Leland, the protagonist in her new book *Tommi Pockets*. Through Tommi, the author reaches out to teens who have to cope with a—to say the least—confusing adult world replete with personal failures and broken families. Like the author, The Salvation Army has a heart for children, and Hubler conveys this deftly as she penetrates the heart of a teen with the promise of redemption young people so need to hear. In so doing, we along with Tommi find that life is more than one big hustle.
—**Jeff McDonald**, Editorial Director, Salvation Army National Publications

Marsha Hubler transports her readers back to the late 1950s to follow the spiritual journey of Tommi Pockets, a teen pool shark who pretends she's a boy to play in a man's world. Cynical, sassy, and troubled, Tommi is drawn to the life of gangs to find the love she craves but can't find at home. Tommi may seem an unlikely Christian model for today's girls, but her journey echoes that of thousands of troubled teens who still roam the streets, end up in juvie, and need a real home. The author shows through this young girl the importance of finding a place to belong in the Body of Christ and the healing grace that comes only from God. This YA novel is a new classic that will change the lives of tweens and teens for years to come.

—**Barbara Scott**, former acquisitions editor for Zonderkidz, Zondervan YA, and Abingdon Fiction

In *Tommi Pockets*, veteran children's novelist Marsha Hubler presents a tale sure to touch young readers. Although set in the simpler times of the late 1950s, the story mirrors today's broken homes and spiritual darkness. No doubt many children who read this compelling story will relate to the dysfunctional Leland family and hear a clear presentation of the gospel for the first time. In answer to the devastation wrought by a society that's largely turned its back on God, Hubler magnificently illustrates Jesus' lifechanging power. Kudos to Hubler on a fine book!

—**Dan Brownell**, editor *Today's Christian Living* and *Today's Pastor*

Looking for a fun book with a wonderful heroine? Tommi Jo, nicknamed Pockets because of her pool expertise, is a girl you want to meet. She's got guts and fire, a great sense of humor, and a soft heart. And has God got plans for her! You can't go wrong spending time with *Tommi Pockets*.

—**Gayle Roper**, award-winning author of *His Plain Truth, Binding Vows*

I rarely read novels. When I was asked to read *Tommi Pockets*, I was a bit skeptical as to whether or not it would be worthwhile reading. I was pleasantly surprised that it was written in first person like an autobiography. By chapter three I was captivated. The story, involving a troubled young teen as the main character, seems so realistic. The redemptive theme begins with the idea based in 2 Corinthians 1:4 that God comforts us in all our tribulation that we may be able to comfort those who are in any trouble. It concludes with salvation and a struggle for Christian growth and a desire to witness to family members. It was a great read; I can't wait for more!

—**Bob Longenecker**, Director, Wayne-Pike Child Evangelism Fellowship, Honesdale, PA

With an authentic voice, humor that is both laugh-out-loud funny and deeply poignant and surprises even the most "bring it on" reader won't see coming, Marsha Hubler makes us wish life really could turn out the way it does for girls like Pockets. And shows us that just maybe it can.

—**Nancy Rue**, best-selling author of over 100 books for young people

Marsha captures the unique nuances between mental health treatment and spiritual discipleship. Her novel, Tommi Pockets, is an empowering story showing the eternal difference one worker makes in a youth's life.

—**Jason P. Lehman** MA, CFLE, NCC—Child Welfare Professional

Marsha Hubler has done it again! *Tommi Pockets* introduces readers to a lonely young girl, forced to masquerade as a boy. Tommi faces every heartbreaking loss and formidable adventure with steely determination. When her grit is put to the ultimate test, she leans on God—and hopes he'll help her meet her greatest challenge yet. Be careful who you loan this one to because you'll want to get it back to read it again. And again!"

—**Loree Lough**, bestselling author of 119 award-winning novels, including reader favorites like *50 Hours* and *A Man of Honor*

TOMMI POCKETS

MARSHA HUBLER

PUBLISHED BY: Elk Lake Publishing, Inc., 35 Dogwood Drive, Plymouth, MA 02360, 2019

Library Cataloging Data

Names: Hubler, Marsha (Marsha Hubler)

Tommi Pockets / Marsha Hubler

172 p. 23cm × 15cm (9in × 6 in.)

Description: Tommi Pockets is a young girl trained by her father as an expert pool player—only she has to disguise herself as a boy to play in the billiard parlors of the day.

Identifiers: ISBN-13: 978-1-951080-05-1 (trade) | 978-1-951080-06-8 (POD) | 978-1-951080-07-5 (e-book)

Key Words: billiards, hustling pool, 1950s, Salvation Army, eight ball, inspirational, middle grade, Ruth McGinnis

LCCN: 2019945150 Fiction

DEDICATION

Dedicated to my friend Nancy, who really did receive a pet alligator from her father.

CHAPTER ONE

ASHLAND, PENNSYLVANIA, 1958

I live with my grandmother. The ugly one.

Mom's mom.

Her name is Mona Heizenroth. I call her Meemaw.

Meemaw thinks she's beautiful. She's paper thin, and she wears a lot of makeup. Her eyelashes look like window shades, and her cheeks look like the number three billiard ball. Even though we don't have the money, she goes to Gracie's Hair Fashions every Friday to get her hair done ... bleached once every three months too! To tell you the truth, that's the only nice thing she allows herself to do with all the bills she has to pay.

My mom's a chip off the old block. She thinks she's beautiful too. That's why she left Pop for another guy a few years ago. She said her new guy looked like Frank Sinatra, her favorite singer. This guy, a jerk, kept telling her she was beautiful with her flaming red, out-of-a-bottle hair and layers of makeup. Mom and him weren't hitched for even a year when he took off with another sucker. Mom said, "Good riddance. He said she was more beautiful than me."

Mom never came home to stay with me, Pop, and Meemaw, even after her second divorce. "I have to explore the world and find the real me," she said, though she only lives on the other side of town in a dumpy apartment. Doesn't seem to me she's explored much of the world, and if she'd look in a mirror, she'd see the real her. I don't see her too often, maybe once a month or so. "I'm holding down three part-time jobs to pay my bills, kid," she tells me. "I don't have much time to myself."

So, why doesn't she come home, and we could all work together to pay the bills?

Pop, my real dad, lives with Meemaw and me … kind of. Sometimes, he disappears for two or three days. We're not sure where he goes, but when he comes back, he's the same as when he left—broke and lookin' awful tired. Maybe it's because his wavy hair that he parts down the middle is almost all white, his wire-framed glasses are all bent out of shape like he is, and he's paper thin, just like Meemaw. Lucky is his nickname, but it sure doesn't match his life. At least he helps pay some of the bills. He does odd jobs like fixing leaky roofs around town, but those jobs are hard to find. For some reason, he can't find steady work with any contractors. And since the coal mines shut down in Pennsylvania, any work is hard to find here.

One thing I know about Pop, though, is I know he loves me because he spends more time with me than anybody else on earth. He even gave me a nickname—Pockets. Yep, just Pop and me. Meemaw doesn't even know what we do when Pop and I go off together.

Meemaw has worked at an envelope factory at the top of town for the last twenty years. She comes home dog tired too but always says, "We need to be thankful I have this job, or we'd be in the poor house."

I'm not sure where that is, but it doesn't sound like any place I'd want to live.

I'm the only offspring of Tom and Nancy Leland. Pop often tells me how they met. "Pockets," he says, "I had just come back from fighting in World War II and was invited to my neighbor's Christmas party. That would be Bertha Stine down on Fifth and

Chestnut. I spotted your mother sitting in a corner all by herself in a ruffled, sparkly, fancy, dark blue dress with her long eyelashes fluttering. I walked over to her, said hi, and three months later, we were hitched. A year later you arrived."

As often as I ask him why I have no brothers or sisters, he always gives me the same answer—"Don't blame me. It's your mother's fault because when she saw you in the hospital, you looked so much like me, she said, 'One of those is enough, thank you.'"

There's not much to say about the rest of our family on either side. Pop never had any brothers or sisters, and the rest of his family lives in Pittsburgh. He never hears from them, but he's never told me why.

As far as Mom's side of the family, she has one sister who lives in Kansas, so they never see each other either. I've never met her. Mom says Aunt Alma has been a widow since the war and has never been the same since her Frank got killed overseas. The only time she's ever contacted any of us is for my birthday. She always sends me a nice card and a little gift. But the gifts are kind of silly, and I think she thinks I'm a boy. One year, she sent three little diecast toy cars. Another time, she sent a toy cap gun. Who knows if I'll get any treasure like that this year. Just so it isn't a Tiny Tears doll.

Here I am thirteen years later, Tommi Jo, the only Leland kid, just squeaked by the seventh grade at Ashland Junior High, not part of the "in" crowd at school, the summer ahead of me, and keeping a secret that no one but Pop can ever know.

"Eight in the corner." I reach under two fake Tiffany-shaded lights and sprawl my scrawny body in a long-sleeved pullover and jeans across the left side of the green pool table. With the precision of a pro, I take deadly aim and smack! The black eight ball flies dead center into a corner pocket and ends the game.

"That's another one for the Leland team," Joe, the official scorekeeper, says.

Cheers from a dozen men fill the back room of Joe's Variety Store in downtown Ashland, dispersing billows of thick cigarette and cigar smoke. I smile and chalk up, ready to break the next rack. Two tired, squeaking ceiling fans mingle the blue haze with a roomful of perspiration on a humid Saturday night in June. From the corner, a jukebox with flashing lights blares the week's top hit, "All I Have to Do is Dream," by the Everly Brothers.

"Way to go, Pockets!" one man shouts over the loud music.

"Keep at it, and you'll be beating Willie Mosconi in a few years," another says.

Pop beams with pride as he scoops up a quarter from the side rail of the table and puffs on his cigar. "That's five games in a row. Not bad at all. That covers more than two hours of time on your table, Joe."

I tug the brim of my Phillies baseball cap down tighter on my forehead, making sure my long blonde hair is tucked tight up inside. Not bad at all … for a girl.

But only Pop knows I'm a girl.

Girls aren't allowed in poolrooms. No, Joe's back room with its one table isn't a "real" poolroom. But the ladies shopping out front wouldn't dare to venture back here, not even to watch. If anyone would ever find out I'm of the female persuasion, I'd be banned from poolrooms forever!

Pop introduced me to the poolroom when I was just four. He plopped a hat on me, put my jacket on backward, and hauled me off to meet his pool buddies. "His head's just screwed on backward," he told them, and they all had a good laugh.

Me? I sat watching those colored balls dance around the table, and I was hooked for life. Couldn't wait until I grew tall enough to reach the table.

My latest victim, Jake Dombroski, makes excuses for his poor game as he slides his fingers through his sweaty black hair and rolls his T-shirt sleeves up over his bulging biceps. "Hey, kid, if I hadn't hurt my arm at the foundry today, you wouldn't have had a run of two. Running all your balls off straight was just plain dumb luck." He takes a long drag on a cigarette and exhales the smoke out his nostrils like a steam engine.

Like vultures stalking a fresh kill, men cackle as they perch on the edge of a row of elevated chairs along the walls. They watch every move I make.

"Jake," a voice yells from the smoky shadows, "just admit you've been whipped by a punk kid still wet behind the ears."

"And one just tall as his stick," another one says. "It's only that baseball cap that gives him a few more inches."

I tug my cap down farther and ease out another discreet smile. "I'm tall enough to reach the table. That's all that counts."

"I know why he's so good." Jake's voice carries a hint of sarcasm. "That Phillies cap keeps out the glare from the lights. Ain't that right, Lucky? Or does your kid have a secret weapon in his hat? He never takes it off!"

Another ripple of laughs breaks out.

"Jake, you ain't nothing but an excuse machine," Pop says. "The Phillies are Tommi's heroes."

"Especially Richie Ashburn!" I add.

Pop adds, "He's just a die-hard Phillies fan. Plain and simple. Any more questions?" He places his cigar in an ashtray, slaps his quarter down on the table rail, and braces his cue. "Quit your yapping and rack 'em up. We've got time for one more game before I have to get home."

I take a quick glance at the clock. Fifteen minutes before midnight. I grab a piece of chalk from the rail and scrape it across my cue. My face burns fire red from the oppressive heat in the small room. "I like the Phillies, that's all," I say as an afterthought. "Plain and simple."

"But you never take off that stupid hat," Jake says. "Nor those long-sleeved shirts. Not even in this oven. We don't even know if you have blond hair like your old man. Is that cap a trademark or something?"

"U.J. Puckett wears a hat all the time when he shoots. Why can't I?" I reach for a can of talcum powder on a shelf in the shadows. I dust my sweaty hands and rub them up and down my stick.

"Pocket's hair's blonde, just like mine was in my younger years," Pop says with a flare of pride. "He's a chip off the old block. Throw in two blue eyes to boot. Question answered. C'mon, let's shoot."

Jake finishes racking the balls and grabs his cue. "Aw right, aw right. So the kid's your carbon copy. But it looks like it won't be long, and he'll pass you by with his shooting. Then you'll be his carbon copy."

Everyone laughed.

"And I welcome that day," Pop brags.

Jake takes another drag on his cigarette and slaps his quarter down. He chalks his cue and squints at a clock in the shadows. "Well, let's see how good you are at midnight. Go ahead and break 'em. I know you always have time for another game … and another two-bits down."

"Count me in!" A familiar voice yells from the doorway of the poolroom.

Runner! I spin toward him, and my heart practically leaps out of my chest.

It's Vince Ramsey, the teen pool shark a grade ahead of me in school. I've had a crush on him ever since he showed up at this poolroom a few months back. Nicknamed "Runner" because of the long runs of balls he can shoot in a row, Vince ranks as one of the top dogs at our neighborhood poolroom on Third and Market. Vince, whose black T-shirt ripples with muscles. His curly hair and dark brown eyes are the dreamiest I've ever seen. I live for the day I can beat him at pool.

But why can't I?

Maybe it's because I can never shoot straight with my heart pounding like a hammer in my throat. Maybe it's because I always find myself staring at him instead of scrutinizing the next shot. Maybe it's because I wonder if I'll ever tell him who I am—what I am.

Yeah, I'd love to beat him at pool. But I love just being near him more.

"Whenever I want you ... all I have to do is dream ... dream ... dream ... dream," blares on the jukebox. And I am dreaming.

I long to tell Runner my secret. I've dreamed a thousand times about yanking off my cap and letting my long hair fall on my shoulders. I want to tell him who I am. What I am. A girl who loves him with every inch of my female being.

I crave love like a bee craves honey. Mom's never around, and I don't ever remember her telling me she loves me. And Pop? Oh, I know he loves me, but sometimes I think it's just because of what I can do with the pool stick—win him quarters for whatever he does with them.

Yes, Meemaw loves me ... I think.

Love? Real love? I feel it when I look into Runner's eyes. If a racing heart and chills up my spine is love, then I know what real love is. Somehow, I have to let him know.

But to Runner, I'm just one of the guys down at the poolroom. And it has to stay that way. Forever. He must never know I'm a girl.

That would end my shooting pool at Joe's or anywhere. It would end my dream to be the first female billiard champ in town—or maybe in the world—when times will change and allow girls in poolrooms. It would also end the only good times I have with Pop when he's shooting pool and not disappearing for days at a time.

Runner must never know. No one must ever know.

"Hey, Runner!" Pop yells. "Let's make it a foursome. Me and the kid will take you and Jake on in a game of straight pool to a hundred." He places another quarter on the rail.

I grab the chalk again and scrape it across my totally worn-out stick. Maybe that's the reason I can't beat Runner. Nah.

Jake plops a quarter down for his new partner. "Come on, Runner. Let's send the Leland team out of here with their tails between their legs."

"The Lelands have won all the marbles for weeks," someone yells from the gallery.

"Yeah, but when Runner and Pockets shoot it out, Runner always buries him," another adds.

"And watch it happen again." Runner retrieves a two-piece pool stick from a small leather case he carries, screws the pieces together, and chalks up. "Tonight the Lelands hit rock bottom."

"Let's just see who'll eat crow pie," Pop says. "Tell you what. We'll give you a head start. You can break 'em."

Runner steps to the head of the table, slides his powerful hands up and down the stick, takes careful aim, and whack! The cue ball sends fifteen colored balls flying all over the table with the red three ball darting into a side pocket.

For the next hour, the pool match between the two best teams at Joe's holds the audience captive. Pop's at his best, running twenty-two balls straight during one shot and fourteen balls in another. But Runner and Jake are out for blood, shooting longer runs that place an easy win in their laps.

And me?

Flustered as I gaze into Runner's eyes, I make five measly balls total and am out of my mind in love.

"Whenever I want you, all I've got to do is dream … dream, dream, dream …."

CHAPTER TWO

"Pop, are we gonna shoot pool tonight?" My dreams of being a pool champ, of Runner, of a better life, help to shut out the loneliness.

It's late Monday morning, and Meemaw is working overtime. She always tells me right before she leaves, "Now remember, Tommi Jo, when I'm away, you're the woman of the house."

I kinda like that. It makes me feel important, somehow, to her and Pop.

Pop shuffles to the coal stove and clears the top of its litter. We're saving for a new electric stove. Maybe next Christmas.

"Don't see why we can't shoot tonight," he says in his tired voice. With a metal poker, he lifts up one of the round iron lids on the stove, tears some shreds of newspaper, throws the paper and a few small slits of wood into the round opening, and lights them with a match. "A hot stove really helps cool off the heat in this kitchen, doesn't it?" he jokes. "But I gotta have my coffee." He replaces the lid, grabs an old tin coffee pot, fills it with water, and goes to a cupboard.

The stove starts to throw a steady low heat, so I take a scoop of small coal pieces the size of raisins from a near-by bucket, lift the stove lid, throw the coal on the kindling fire, and replace the lid. "Pop, what do you want for breakfast? A couple of eggs? I'll make them for you."

"Nah, I ain't hungry." Pop opens the cupboard and pulls out a canister. He scoops coffee into the tin pot and places the pot on the stove. "I'll just have some jelly bread. You better get busy cleaning up the house so it's nice for your grandma when she gets home. You know she doesn't like to come home to a dirty house."

"Can we go to Joe's then for sure?" I attack the mountain of dirty dishes in the sink.

"As soon as you have the house cleaned up." Pop opens the refrigerator door and peeks in. "Those quarters we'll earn will come in handy for some bread and milk."

The rest of the day I go through my Monday routine—cleaning our run-down row house at 1809 Market Street. I scrub the kitchen from top to bottom and pile bags of garbage out on the front sidewalk for early pick up. I do two loads of wash in Meemaw's beat-up wringer washer, including hanging the clothes on our wash lines in the back yard. For supper, I make Poor Man's Stew, a watery blend of potatoes, carrots, celery, and onions. Every minute of the long day, I plan my future as the First Woman World Billiard Champ … with Runner by my side, dreaming and scheming about a better tomorrow. Someday I'll be gone from Ashland. Forever. And no one will miss me. Not even my teachers.

Teachers?

Teachers at W.C. Estler Elementary never noticed I needed help. Three Ds and an F on my sixth grade report card? C'mon, people! Get with it! If they did notice, they didn't seem to care. The teachers at junior high are all the same. No help at all. Although Miss Williams, my history teacher, told me once that I have a good mind, and if I'd use it, I could be an "A" student. One of these days, I think I will start using my mind for school work, not that it'll help me at all win the billiard championship. As far as teachers prying into my private life, it's better if they don't know much about me, Meemaw, and Pop. Snooping teachers will probably just make things worse.

What about all my friends?

Who needs them? Friends visit each other's homes. I don't want anyone to see how I live. Friends ask questions I know I can't, or don't want to, answer.

I'm on my own. I have to help myself, to make my own life. I have to keep shooting pool and getting better and better. To become the champ. The prize money from all the matches is my way out … someday.

But then there are the Thorns. I guess it's time to let you know I have more than one secret.

Monday at dusk, I push my aching body to its limits, hurrying to the corner of Third and Market. Only minutes ago, I left Meemaw sound asleep on the couch. At her age, the overtime is starting to get to her. She won't wake up until tomorrow morning. Now, to catch my breath, I stop in front of Joe's, where Pop and I will not be shooting pool tonight. He's gone again … who knows where? And for how long this time? More promises broken. Probably tying one on at Malloney's.

I pause at the poolroom doorway and listen to a barrage of laughter and the smack of pool balls. The jukebox blares "You ain't nothin' but a hound dog" in true Elvis Presley style. I ache to go inside, to join the fun, to see Runner, but without Pop I'm an uninvited guest. He's got the cash.

I turn away, hurry around the corner, and cross onto Second Street, slipping into a narrow alley already draped in nine-o'clock shadows. I tug my cap into its proper place and head down three more blocks to the edge of town toward my other life, the one I keep secret—even from Pop.

As I run, I think back to a few minutes ago at home—how I prepared for this next rendezvous. I donned a washed-off blue jean jacket that matches my pants. My neck now proudly displays a bright purple kerchief. The sleeve of my coat boasts a patch with a purple rose encased in a web of briars and the name "THORNS" embroidered in bold black letters. Despite my aching legs from the run, I smile. I can't wait to join those who wait just ahead.

Panting like a rabid dog from the summer heat, the heavy clothes, and exhausting run, I approach the back entrance to a deserted brick factory shell. I turn, survey the shadows for any sign of unwelcomed life, and sneak up to a battered steel door shut tight. Again, I study the shadows, tap the door three times, wait, then tap twice and wait again.

The door squeaks, barely opening. Through the thin slit, I see an eye. I know it's Bowser's eyeball. Bowser's the lookout.

"What's the password?" his gruff whisper demands.

"Rumble," I whisper back.

The door cracks open enough to let me squeeze through, then closes quietly.

Across the humongous dark, musty room I follow Bowser, his clothes a carbon copy of mine except his head is wrapped in a purple bandana. I fix my gaze on a corner straight ahead, on a dim yellow glow offering the only light in the entire place. I take a deep, relaxed breath. I feel at peace, at home. To me, this is home.

Goyne's Mine Pump Company. The old shell had long ago lost the glory of its thriving, world-wide business. Now deserted and left to its own demise, the building fills most the run-down part of town. But not a soul on the planet cares if the once-stately structure stands or falls. No one cares but gutter rats and about a dozen neighborhood ruffians.

Approaching the light, my heart races and my nerves are unsteady. I take another deep breath, and my lungs fill with stuffy air saturated with the fumes of stale oil and rotting floorboards. Although I'm sweating like a greased pig, I feel a chill up my spine. I've been granted entrance to the hallowed ground of Slick Garside and the gang members who control the East Side.

I follow Bowser to the "headquarters," an office in its better days, where a meeting of the Thorns is already under way. Focusing on Slick, I slip in and stand behind a semicircle of boys sitting on overturned buckets and crates listening to their bossman who stands before them. Bowser joins the circle and lights up a cigarette. Smoke from several others has already clouded the small room, making the oppressive air even harder to breathe. One rusty oil lamp on top of a rustier file cabinet throws off just enough light to carry on the business at hand.

"Pockets, you're late," Slick says with a half-smile.

"Sorry," I reply. "My grandmother had me—"

"Don't let it happen again!" Slick's demeanor changes, and he spews out the words while yanking a comb from inside his black leather jacket smothered in decorative chains. Starting at his long sideburns, he slicks back his black hair. His heavily greased ducktail now perfected, its shine takes center stage even in the dingy light. "Park yourself somewhere," he orders.

"It won't happen again," I promise. I slide quickly onto a vacant crate and cross my arms.

Slick shoves the comb back into his jacket and slouches into a wooden chair that has seen better days. He props his ankle on his knee, displaying one of his black motorcycle boots that's trying its best to outshine his hair. "We've got to do something about the Hawks," he says. "They're invading our turf east of Fourth and Vine. They need to know who's boss in these parts— and now!"

Bowser blows out a long drag of smoke. "Snitch said they beat up the Scorpions pretty bad in their rumble last week on the North Side. The Hawks suddenly inherited twelve more blocks of that turf."

Again, Slick reaches inside his jacket, this time pulling out a pack of Lucky Strikes and a lighter. He lights up, flips the lighter shut, and jams it and the pack inside his coat. With the cigarette dangling from his lips, he leans back, locks his hands behind his head, and stares straight ahead. Everyone sits, waiting.

I scrutinize every detail in the dingy room. With a flush of pride, I study each member of the gang, about a dozen guys, which I've been a part for the last two years. Bowser, Butch, Charlie, Thumper—I know all of them well. Each hardened face focuses intently on our leader. All their homes are like mine, let's just say, with "messed up" parents and such monstrous problems, they have no time for anyone else, even their own flesh and blood.

I know these guys. I grew up with these homeboys on the street and went to school with many of them before they quit and made the gang their life. Now they're showing me, their fledgling, how running with a gang is done.

I half-smile. These boys do know who I am, what I am. A girl. But they don't care. I am one of them. Just like every other Thorn, I've done my share of dirt as a wannabe—slashing tires, breaking windows, stealing from the butcher. I made it "in" on my own. Finally, I'm ready to move up to the next notch. Now, I've earned the right to rumble.

My glance darts back to Slick.

Big shot Slick. Only by his graces and a thumbs-up vote from the gang did I get in. Childhood friendships and hood loyalties have allowed me to do something that no other female would ever do—rumble with the Thorns and become a bona fide member.

Slick shifts his glance to the ceiling and studies it like he's reading the book, Hateful Ways to Get Even. He takes a long drag on his cigarette, blows three perfect rings into the air, and shoves the cigarette back between his lips. Lost in his stare, he folds his arms while his boot pumps to a phantom beat.

"Slick—" Bowser starts to say.

His stare fixed, Slick raises a palm toward Bowser. "I'm thinkin'. I'm thinkin'."

Silence.

Slick takes another drag and blows out a long, gray billow. Finally, he speaks. "Yeah, they need to know who's boss in these parts, and now. Butch, what's the lowdown on the Scorpions?"

My glance shifts to a hefty boy sitting on an overturned coal bucket. Long sideburns protrude from each side of the purple kerchief that covers what I know is a crop of curly red hair. His face, fiery red and moist from the stifling heat, is splattered with freckles.

"They're thirteen strong right now," he reports. "They lost two from broken arms in their rumble with the Hawks."

Tap, tap, tap.

Tap, tap.

Bowser scrambles off his crate and hurries out of the room.

Slick takes one last suck on his smoke. "Snitch will give us the lowdown on the Hawks. He was visiting them today."

In seconds, Bowser rushes into the room and sits. On his heels comes a tall, thin boy dressed in a yellow T-shirt and brown pants, trying to catch his breath. Horn-rimmed glasses and a spiked crewcut complete his nerdy look. I always thought his look's the closest thing to an owl in human flesh I've ever seen.

Slick stands, his eyes burning with hateful revenge. "What's the scoop?"

"The Hawks are thirteen strong," Snitch says. "No casualties from their clash with the Scorpions. They plan to invade our turf tonight with two dozen cans of red spray paint, starting at midnight in Eureka Park."

"Well, we'll just see about that." Slick's flaming eyes shift to me. "Pockets, are you ready?"

My nerves jump me to my feet. "Yes, sir. I'm ready."

"Then we're eleven strong," Slick says confidently. "With an extra swinging bat, we can take 'em. Snitch, get word to those scuzz buckets that they better stay clear of Eureka Park and this whole East Side, or they're gonna pay big time."

"Yes, sir." Snitch turns and hurries out.

"Thorns!" Slick says with a sinister grin plastered on his face.

Like Marines in boot camp, every boy stands. "Yes, sir!" they yell.

"Tonight we rumble!" Slick declares.

"Tonight we rumble!" we all yell back.

CHAPTER THREE

Armed with baseball bats, the eleven of us hunker down behind a hedgerow bordering the west boundary of Eureka Park. Our park! I'm stationed between Slick and Bowser, squinting in the dark, watching for any sign of movement. I'm nervous as a kitten in a bubble bath. Half of me because I'm a chicken scared out of my wits, the other half excited to be part of something-big scared out of my wits.

The only things moving in the park are four swings swaying in the gentle summer breeze. My gaze sweeps the entire park—the water fountain nestled in its little red brick gazebo, the towering sliding board, the monkey bars. On the left, I spot the tiny kids' merry-go-round, the four long pavilions of picnic tables. To the right, about a third of a football field away, the bandstand with its three tin walls and overhang ... all dead silent. The only help for me to see anything comes from dull light bulbs, maybe a dozen of them, hanging sparsely from a web of wires all over the park.

"There!" I whisper. "I just saw something moving on the left side of the bandstand."

"I saw it too," Slick whispers. "And I'm sure I saw red! They're staked out behind the bandstand. I can feel it in my bones."

"Slick, what do you wanna do?" Bowser whispers.

"Let's get them," Butch says, "before they start marking their territory."

"No," Slick says. "Wait 'til they make their move. My gut's telling me they're going to spray the bandstand walls. Then we'll surround them."

I watch in stiff silence, grasping my bat so tight my fingers cramp. Beads of sweat drip down my forehead, and I wipe them on my sleeve. In seconds, I see shadowy figures, one at a time, sneaking from behind the bandstand and climbing up on its cement platform. I do a quick count. Only twelve Hawks! We can take them, I think.

"Let's go," Slick says. "Bowser, you and your four take the left side, and I'll take the right side with my five. When I yell, 'Let's rumble!' charge them and start swinging."

We sneak toward the bandstand, and I'm shaking so bad I almost wet myself. As we creep within a stone's throw of our targets, my stare is glued on the bandstand. I watch as the Hawks sneak toward the walls with cans of spray paint in one hand and baseball bats in the other.

"Let's rumble!" Slick yells to the top of his lungs.

"Let's rumble!" we all yell and charge the bandstand.

Caught off guard, the Hawks drop their cans and lunge at us with their bats swinging. Obscenities from both sides boom through the night air as we clash. I follow in Bowser's footsteps with my bat cocked, looking for a red kerchief. Bowser swings and hits a Hawk in the middle of the punk's back. The Hawk screams and falls to the ground. I raise my bat to swing at him when suddenly, I'm hit on my right arm, and pain shoots through my body like nothing I've ever felt before. I scream and drop my bat while Bowser covers my tail.

Scr-ree-ree-ree-ree-ree! Cop car sirens cut through the chaos, and before we know it, we're all surrounded by an army of blue uniforms pointing lead in our faces. We're rounded up like pigs off to the slaughter and packed into two of our own private paddy wagons. And that was a smart move by the cops, or us gangs would have killed each other. Then we're hauled off to the police station.

Some know-it-all fuzz herds us Thorns into "the tank," a large, dingy room with nothing but dilapidated folding chairs hugging the faded green walls. It's my guess the Hawks are somewhere just feet away in their tank. Slick and the boys throw out a string of insults at the fuzz and slouch in their chairs. They've all been here before. They know the routine, so they relax against the wall and close their eyes. Butch has a bloody mouth, but everyone else came through the battle unscathed.

Me? I sit next to Bowser, erect in my chair with my nerves playing Tiddly Winks with my muscles. My wounded arm is killing me. I try to nurse it into a comfortable position, knowing that by now it's a big, swollen blotch of black and blue. The only thing on any wall is a clock. I stare at it mercilessly for hours.

Nothing happens until three a.m. when Sergeant Know-It-All comes in, points his finger at me, and says, "You! Come with me!" He's a huge beast of a man, his brown hair in a crewcut and his wide, black leather belt loaded with a pistol, handcuffs, a billy club, and keys. Who'd wanna mess with this cop?

I'm led to another large room, this one a little brighter, crowded with a clutter of desks all over the room. The desks, weighed down with typewriters and mounds of files and papers, sit silent except for two in the farthest corner next to a second door. I focus on those farthest desks. Sitting next to each desk is a Hawk. At each typewriter, a cop is typing away.

"Sit here!" The fuzz says to me and points to a chair beside the desk to my immediate right. He stations himself behind the desk and feeds a paper into the typewriter. "What's your name, kid?" he growls.

"Tommi Jo Leland, and … can I use the bathroom?" I blurt out although it's already too late.

"In a little while," he says. "I'm Officer Bailey, kid. I need to get some information down here, so we can contact your folks. Give me their names and your address. Don't you think they'll be wondering where you are at three o'clock in the morning?"

"I live with my mee—my grandmother and my pop. She's sleeping off twelve hours of overtime, and I don't know if Pop's home or not. He disappears sometimes. He might be at Malloney's Bar."

"Okay, Tommi," he says with a kinder tone. "Let's get some questions answered, and we'll try to get hold of them to come for you."

"I-I'm not going to juvey hall or jail?"

He types as fast as I talk. "No. The rest of your gang's getting sent away, but it looks like this is your first offense. You're squeaking through this time, but the next time you won't be so lucky."

I watch the clock on the wall as the next hour drags by. I answer question after question, but he never once asks me if I'm a girl. My hat is in its pulled-down-fool-everybody place, and my hair is tucked up and plastered tight with sweat against my head so that not one blonde strand has gone AWOL. The only thing he questions is my age. "You're only thirteen? Kid, what are you doing running with such a gang of losers?"

I almost let it fly to tell him to mind his own business, but I just sit with my lips buttoned shut. I do a Thorns slouch with my arms crossed and stare at the floor.

"Okay, kid. I think we're done here. We'll take you to the restroom and then back to the tank until somebody comes to pick you up." He points his chubby finger at me. "And keep your nose clean. I don't want to see you here again, or you will be heading to reform school."

"You mean that's it? I don't have to serve any time at all?"

"Not in lock-up. But we're sending you to the Salvation Army."

"The Salvation Army? What am I? An old shirt nobody wants?"

Sergeant Know-It-All laughs. He actually laughs out loud! "Hey, kid, that's a good one." He relaxes back into his chair and places his hands behind his head. "You're going to have three months of counseling with a social worker at the Army's headquarters downtown. Twice a week, and you better show up!"

"You've got to be kidding. I'm going to see a shrink?"

He laughs again. "No, it's nothing like that. Arlene is a counselor, not a psychiatrist. She just talks to kids and tries to help them with their home life, school, friends. I think you'll like her. She's one tough cookie. She knows kids inside and out."

I say nothing. It's hard to talk when you're in shock. No way do I want to spill my guts to some religious weirdo in a starched uniform.

"Any questions?" the officer asks as he leans forward, ready to type.

I shake my head while I stare holes through him.

He stands. "Okay then. Let's get you settled. C'mon."

I stand to walk out and take one last glance at the back of the room that for the last hour resembled a busy bus station. Just as I turn to leave, I spot another red kerchief being led out in handcuffs. No, it can't be! He's a Hawk?

It's Runner!

To say Meemaw and Pop were upset when the police finally caught up with them about me being busted is way off base by a zillion miles.

Eight o'clock Tuesday morning, Meemaw finally answers the phone, and by nine, I'm at our kitchen table with her sitting across from me with fire in her mascaraed eyes and Pop screaming his lungs out at me. I sit with my ball cap and purple kerchief on in my official Thorns slump with my arms crossed even though my injured arm pulsates fire. I make up my mind to say nothing to incriminate myself.

"Tommi Jo Leland, how long has this gang business been going on with you? And take that stupid purple kerchief off!" Pop leans on the table cleared of everything but a few crumbs and a bunch of papers from the police. Pop wags his index finger a few inches from my nose. A wave of liquor breath hits me square in the face. I know he's really, really ticked at me because the last time he called me by my full name was when I was six and started a kitchen fire trying to cook my own oatmeal on the stove.

I stare at a fly helping itself to the crumbs and say nothing. I take my good old time pulling off my kerchief. I might as well kiss it goodbye. My gang days are over, for sure.

"Tommi Jo, this is your father speaking. Look at me." He touches the tip of my nose.

I am so glad he let me know he's my father. I decide to look at him to avoid what might happen next if I ignore him. He could give me a good thrashing like he did with the oatmeal incident. Right now, I can hardly stand the pain in my arm, let alone imagine my butt burning like fire too.

"Answer your father," Meemaw says, her face draped in a strange combination of anger and disappointment. Even at this time of the morning, she's got her layers of makeup on. I guess she wanted to look presentable at the police station.

"Do you want to be grounded for the rest of the summer?" Pop stands erect, crosses his arms, and waits.

I doubt he really means that. If I'm grounded that long, he'll be hurting more than me. Who'll help him win all those quarters at Joe's? "No, I don't want to be grounded all summer."

"Well?" he snaps.

"You know all those guys," I say. "They're all kids I grew up with here in the neighborhood. You know Slick, ah that's Harry Garside, and Bowser, and Butch, and—"

"And when did all of this turn into a stupid gang?" he asks. "The policeman said the rest of them are all being sent to reform school. They'll be gone upstate for at least a year. You are one lucky kid. They're giving you a second chance."

"That's what the fuzz told me," I say.

"Policeman," Meemaw says. "He's a policeman."

For the next half hour or so, they both rant and rave about how ungrateful I am to have a nice home, and what am I doing running around with such punks. Never mind that I've been up all night in the tank with just a few catnaps, and my arm's killing me. I still don't know if Pop was home when the fuzz called or not. Nevertheless, as Pop reads me the riot act, my mind drifts to last night ... Slick and the boys ... are they already on their way to reform school? And Runner. What happened to him? Will I ever see him again? My heart aches more than my arm.

"Okay, Tommi Jo," Pop says, interrupting my dark thoughts. "You're not going anywhere for a week except to see that counselor downtown. Not anywhere else for one whole week. Do you hear me?"

"What do you have to say about that?" Meemaw says as she pushes away from the table and hobbles to the refrigerator. "I'll get us some scrambled eggs going."

What am I supposed to say? Yippee Doodle? Well, I feel like it 'cause I probably do deserve a lot worse, but Pop needs me. It's probably harder for him to stay away from the poolroom than it is for me. And Meemaw will know if I've been home all week by the way the house will look. Grandmas just know those things.

Me? I feel like jumping up and down with joy. Only a week? What a break.

CHAPTER FOUR

The next Tuesday at nine a.m. sharp, Pop takes me in our '53 pea-green Chevy to Post 71, the Salvation Army's hangout in a downtown storefront. The post is sandwiched between the Ashland Fire Hose Company and Woolworth's general store.

Pop made me take a bath before my week was up, but he didn't care what I wore, so I've got on my Phillies cap with my hair tucked in place and my favorite blue jeans, the knees worn through, but the cleanest jeans I have. The monstrous goony on my arm can't get any blacker and bluer than it is, so I wear my long-sleeved beat-up blue Phillies pullover, just to avoid a lot of questions.

It's a perfect, warm June morning with a gentle breeze, the kind I like to spend hanging out at one of the three town parks, looking for anyone who could become my friend. But here I go, stuck in some lousy building listening to some other know-it-all lecturing me how to run my life.

Pop pokes the doorbell, as the little sign says to do. We go in and sit in a stuffy waiting room a lot like our doctor's office. But this room's smaller with only six empty wooden chairs hugging the walls. In one corner rests a beat-up coffee table with a small stack of magazines. The walls are a faded yellow, dressed up with about a dozen framed pictures of people in starched navy blue uniforms. The men with their hats look like they're ready to go off to war, and the women with big bonnets look like they're going off to church. I figure they're probably all big shots that run the outfit. The linoleum floor has a faded tan brick design. Everything is worn out—spotless clean but worn out.

My gaze shifts to the back of the room with a closed door in dead center. We sit and wait for about fifteen minutes. Pop doesn't say boo, grabs a magazine, pokes back his glasses, and focuses on the magazine. I study all the corny pictures on the walls and wonder how anyone in his right mind could be a "soldier" in the Salvation Army. Who are they fighting anyway?

The door opens, and out comes a not-too-thin woman, thirty maybe, in her starched-to-beat-the-band navy blue uniform minus the bonnet. The woman has wavy blonde hair drawn back in a bun and the bluest eyes I've ever seen. Penetrating eyes. I thought I had blue eyes! I don't detect any makeup, but her face somehow seems to glow with pure joy. If she ever fought in any wars, I just know she won them all. Her jacket's got shiny gold buttons, and her skirt is ironed to perfection and goes to her shins. Her black shoes look like the kind Meemaw wears to work, with laces and really thick soles.

Pop closes his magazine, and we both stand.

"Good morning," she says with a welcoming smile that reveals a set of perfect teeth. Her bluest of eyes focus on me. "Are you Tommi Jo Leland?"

"Yeah," I say almost in a whisper.

Her attention shifts to Pop. "Mr. Leland?"

"Yes," he says in his nervous voice.

"Wonderful," she says and shakes my father's hand. "I'm Arlene Masters. Mr. Leland, these sessions are going to take about an hour-and-a-half. If you'd like to leave and come back for Tommi, that will be fine with me."

"Well," he says, "I do have some things to do, so I'll come back around ten thirty."

I wonder what he has to do.

"Great," she says as she extends her hand toward me, inviting me to go with her.

My first panicked thought is to wrap my arms and legs around Pop and scream, "Don't leave me here alone with this woman!" Then I entertain the idea of just splitting, but that would get me sent to reform school quicker than I can count to ten, so I bite the bullet and decide to stay.

"I think Tommi and I are going to get along just fine," she says, turning toward the opened door. "C'mon, Tommi. We've got a lot to discuss."

I follow the woman beyond the opened door, picturing myself going to the guillotine. I hear the front door close and know Pop's gone, and I'm at the mercy of this woman.

"Welcome to my office," she says as she sits behind a worn-out wooden desk overloaded with files and a typewriter. "Have a seat." She points to a metal folding chair stationed right in front of her desk. While she shuffles some papers, I scan the room. It is almost a carbon copy of the waiting room even with another door in the center of the wall behind the desk. But this room has pictures on the walls of really neat mountains, waterfalls, and sunsets. Some of the pictures have sayings on them. One has the words "I can do all things through Christ which strengtheneth me." I have no idea what that ancient language means.

The woman opens a file, folds her hands on top, and smiles at me. "It's customary for a young man to take off his hat in the presence of a lady. Would you please remove yours?"

Boing! She thinks I'm a boy. Yes! And so did Sergeant Know-It-All. He checked my file as MALE. I can't let this secret out! I slouch, cross my arms, and stare at the floor.

Silence.

"I have hours of work that will keep me busy," she finally says, "but your father will be back at ten thirty. I wonder how long he'll be prepared to sit and wait until you take your hat off."

I stare at the floor, wondering how I'm going to get out of this mess. I sit and listen as she works on her precious files, shuffling papers, opening and closing desk drawers, typing. I sit, probably for at least a half hour or so. I feel my face flush red hot with rage, but I'm dead sunk like a mouse in a trap. I can't take it any longer, so I rip off my Phillies cap. My long hair falls freely to my shoulders, and I stare at her with utter contempt.

"Well, well, well," she says, relaxing back into her chair. "We have a 'Miss' Tommi Jo." She gives me one of those disgusting smiles again. "It's nice to know you, Miss Leland."

I scowl at her and spew out, "If they ever find out I'm a girl at Joe's, my days of shooting pool with Pop are over. He counts on those quarters we win 'cause he doesn't work much. And everybody calls me 'Pockets.'"

"I see. Well, I'm not going to run right down there and tell Joe you're a girl," she says in such a convincing tone I actually think she means it. "Tommi, I mean, Pockets, I want you to know you can trust me. You can tell me anything, and that information goes no further. The only exception involves your grandma and father. If you share with me some issues that involve them, we might have some family powwows to resolve the problem. But I'd first discuss with you the possibility of a family meeting. We have no nasty "gotcha" surprises here at Post 71. Understand?"

I just nod and stare at her blue eyes. I almost feel buck naked when she looks at me, like she already knows every teensy weensy detail about me since I was born and wants to "fix" me. I bet she even knows how many times I've stuffed string beans in my socks at supper time because I hate them so much.

She picks up a paper from a file, focuses for a few seconds, then looks at me. "Pockets, since you've told me your nickname already, how about if I share with you what I'd like you to call me. The kids that hang out here call me 'Captain Ar.' How does that sit with you?"

I shrug. "Okay, I guess. Are you a real captain?" For some reason, all of a sudden I feel like talking to this woman.

She throws out a quick smile. "Yes, I've been here for twelve years and have worked my way up to that level."

"Did you have to fight in any wars?" After I say that, I think how stupid a question it is.

"No," she says with a wider smile, almost a stifled laugh. "Most of the time, the labels like 'captain,' 'sergeant,' and 'general' are only indications of the time we've served here or the jobs we've done. The Salvation Army isn't a 'war' kind of army, Pockets. Our battles are for the souls of men—to save folks, not kill them. You'll get to understand that better as time goes on."

I just nod again, not understanding at all what she just said. Then I remember she said something about kids. "What other kids come here?"

She lays down the paper and relaxes back into her chair. "That's a good question, Pockets. We have about a dozen kids in counseling right now. Most of them come twice a week like you will be doing. You might even know some of them from school. If not, you'll get to know them, if you'd like to. That is, if you'd like to come to our Friday Fun Nights." She yanks her thumb over her shoulder. "Behind this door is a room full of interesting things like table games, a dart board, a ping-pong table, and something I'm sure you'll love."

My heart skips a beat, and I almost jump out of my chair. "A pool table?"

"Um-m, maybe," she says with a wink and a smile. "If you come faithfully for your sessions with me, you'll get to see what's behind this back wall."

Now I'm more interested than ever to hang out with this woman.

She takes a quick glance at the file on the desk. "I see here that your birthday's coming up next week, and you'll be fourteen."

"Yeah," I say with no enthusiasm.

"Do your folks have a party for you or do anything special?"

"Nah, not really. I don't have any friends from school, and Mom's always working. I only see her once in a while. She's too busy to come to a dumb old party. Meemaw, that's my grandma, usually cooks for supper whatever I want if she doesn't have to work overtime. If she does work, then Pop and I go to Sebastians' Cafe for a hamburger, then go to Joe's to clean up a whole bunch of quarters. I really don't mind 'cause I love to shoot pool with Pop. One day I'm going to be champ and win a whole bunch of money."

"Is that your dream, Pockets?"

"As long as I can remember. And Pop says I'm getting better all the time. All we have to do is wait, or maybe try to do something, so that girls are allowed to play pool."

"Yes, that is a big problem, isn't it?"

I look beyond her, wondering if there is a pool table in that other room.

"And, yes, there is a pool table back there, and girls are allowed to use it. But you have to earn that right."

"How?" I ask, my heart racing like a horse at the finish line.

"You'll find out in good time … all in good time," she says with that sickening smile.

Another hot and sunny Monday morning, June 28th—my birthday—and, as usual, nobody cares that much. I ask Meemaw if I can have a birthday cake, but she says she doesn't have time to bake one. She does say she'll make my favorite meal for supper—spaghetti with big-as-the-moon meatballs, cinnamon apple sauce (in a jar from the Acme Market), and chocolate milk (from the same store). I can't wait until supper.

I ask Pop if we'll be shooting tonight.

He says, "I think so. I know that's what you'd like to do on your birthday. I have a small job helping someone fix a garage roof down on Brock Street. I should be home in plenty of time for supper … and pool."

So I'm counting on doing that with him after supper.

All morning, I help Meemaw do the dishes, scrub the kitchen floor, and hang up a load of wash. I grab a quick sandwich for lunch then take off.

"Be back in plenty of time for supper!" she yells as I slam the screen door, hop on my Roadmaster bike, and head toward the Higher Ups Park. I figure I didn't do so well at Eureka Park the last time I went there. The fuzz might still be staking out the place, so I avoid that park like poison ivy and go for Plan B on my special day. And I'll be home long before supper. I wouldn't miss Meemaw's spaghetti for anything this side of the Atlantic Ocean.

I know that any neighborhood kids who aren't at reform school are probably playing baseball at the Higher Ups Park. I only take ten minutes to get there on my bike. My bike's seven years old but still kicking.

Scoping the ballfield, I see a game going on that will last most of the afternoon. I park my bike, grab a quick drink of water from the fountain, and sit on the empty bleacher to watch the game. Me and that game never did get along. When I was about eight and just learning how to play, I took a baseball right between my eyes. From that day on, me and the game of baseball went our separate ways, at least, as far as me playing. But I still love to watch the Phillies on TV, especially Richie Ashburn.

A few of the kids look my way, and Leona Kaminski gives a quick wave. I wave back, knowing that's as far as our friendship will ever go. She only lives one street away from me, but our interests are as different as black and white. She's a real looker with long dark curls—the cheerleader type. She gets good grades, loves sports, and is part of the "in" crowd. Of all the kids in that crowd, she's the only one who ever even acknowledges that I'm a living being, not a rock. Maybe someday …

I've got my faithful cap on and my hair all tucked away, but it really doesn't matter. All these neighborhood kids know I'm a girl. Their world and the world I share with Pop at midnight will never cross paths. Even if any of their dads ever went to Joe's to shoot pool, which none have ever done, they'd never put two and two together. I've never been to one of their homes anyway, so they don't know me from a fire hydrant. They don't have a clue about the Thorns, either. What they don't know won't hurt them.

As I sit there, I study every one of them playing their game. I know them all pretty well, but they don't know me at all. I wonder what it would be like to have a lot of friends, to have them come to a surprise birthday party for me and give me really nice gifts. I just sit and wonder.

I hang around and watch the game until about four o'clock. I've learned to tell the time by spotting where the sun is in the sky and how hot the air feels. It's too early to go home, so I decide to ride downtown and just take a peek at the Salvation Army post. Just because.

Last Friday, I got drilled by "Captain Ar." For an hour-and-a-half straight, all that woman did was ask question after question while she typed up a blue streak. I'd like to know when the stupid "counseling" is supposed to start.

I stop right in front of the Woolworth's store and pretend I'm looking at the window display. Out of the corner of my eye, I focus on the post's door, wondering if Captain Ar is in there. I wait about a half hour or so, but nobody goes in or comes out until finally the door opens, and out comes the woman in her starched uniform.

I turn and grab my bike as if I don't see her and make like I'm going to take off.

"Pockets!" she says loud enough so anyone within a mile can hear her.

I turn and act like I'm totally surprised I'd ever see her there. "Oh, hi."

She closes the post's door and makes sure it's locked. "What are you doing down here this time of the day?"

I sit on my bike, ready to split. "Oh, nothing. Just goofin' off."

"Well, it's good to see you, young lady," she says. "Listen, I'd love to stay and chat, but I've got an appointment. Will I see you here at nine o'clock sharp tomorrow morning?"

"Yeah," I say in my perfectly bored voice. She's the first person to ever call me "young lady."

"See you then," she says and starts walking the opposite direction. I wonder where she lives, if she has a car, a husband, any kind of a life outside of the Salvation Army. I make up my mind the next time I see her to ask her a zillion questions. I watch as she walks to the end of the block, turns right, and disappears around the corner. I check my "sky clock" and air temperature and figure it's past suppertime, so I start peddling like crazy toward home, my mouth watering just thinking about Meemaw's spaghetti.

In about fifteen minutes, I pull into my back yard, park the bike, hang my cap on the handlebars, and hurry into the kitchen, hoping my few late minutes didn't tick off Meemaw or Pop.

"Surprise!" echoes through the room, and I'm shocked almost out of my socks at who is here.

CHAPTER FIVE

My stupid mouth falls open as I stare at Pop smiling and wearing a black bow tie and a T-shirt that looks like a tuxedo with his gray work pants. Meemaw's smiling to beat the band with an extra layer of makeup on and a frilly pink apron covering her navy blue polka-dotted house dress. She's holding a big two-layer birthday cake with chocolate icing and candles blazing away, and to her left stands the woman!

Captain Ar is here. She's actually in my house in "people" clothes—a plain tan blouse and a brown and yellow-striped pleated skirt. Nobody would know she's a captain in those duds. I can't believe it, but she, Meemaw, and Pop are all wearing ridiculous birthday hats that look like unicorn horns.

I feel a little embarrassed with the crumby, sweaty clothes I have on. I guess the word "surprise" is excuse enough.

Meemaw positions the cake on the one end of the table already set with four place settings of birthday paper plates and cups. I look at the counter next to the refrigerator and spot three gifts wrapped in fancy birthday paper and another funny-looking brown package not quite the size of a shoe box with tiny holes haphazardly poked through it.

I just stand there like a big dummy, staring.

"Well, say something." Meemaw hurries to me, grabs my hand, and pulls me to the table.

"I-I-," I squeak out as I survey the whole situation again and rivet my stare on Captain Ar. What is she doing here? And why?

"Sit down, everyone," Meemaw says as she heads to the stove. "Spaghetti and meatballs coming up."

"May I help you with anything, Mona?" Captain Ar asks as she throws her signature smile at me.

"No, it's all ready," Meemaw says. "Please have a seat."

"It's so nice to have you here with us," Pop says to Captain Ar as the three of us sit at the table. His voice is quivering a little, like he's nervous or something.

"Well, thank you for inviting me," she says as she picks up a birthday napkin and places it on her lap.

Pop puts his napkin on his lap. That's the first time I've ever seen him do that. He tries to start a conversation. "The way Pockets has been talking about you, we figured she'd love to have you here."

Now wait a minute. I've hardly said beans to anyone about the woman. Where'd he get such an idea that I'd want her here? On second thought, it really is nice to have someone visit us, even if it is her. And on my birthday, no less.

Meemaw carries a huge pot of spaghetti from the stove and sets it in the center of the table. I spot apple sauce in a fancy dish and a quart of chocolate milk already settled in on the table.

"Would you like coffee, Arlene?" Meemaw asks.

"Yes, thank you," she says.

Meemaw brings the coffee pot to the table and pours three cups while I fill my birthday cup up to its brim with chocolate milk.

For the next who-knows-how-long, we eat the best spaghetti in all the world and top it off with Meemaw's chocolate cake. I hardly say boo while the others discuss the weather, President Eisenhower and the state of the nation's affairs, and the grim possibility of the mines ever opening again in central Pennsylvania. While I eat, I stare ... mostly at the woman,

wondering what makes her tick. For the first time since I've met
her, I notice she's not wearing a wedding ring. So her total life
must be the Salvation Army. I can't put my finger on it, but
there's something different about her—so very, very different. I
have to find out what that is. I like it. I want it.

We finish supper, clear the table, and set the leftovers on the
counter by the sink while Pop carries the four gifts to the table.
"Well, Pockets, it's time to see what's in these curious packages."

We gather around the table, and as embarrassed as I am to
be doing this kids' stuff in front of the woman, my heart races,
wondering what treasures await me.

Meemaw picks up a flat box about the size of a clipboard
wrapped in really cool birthday paper with bright colored
balloons all over it. Captain Ar stands with her arms crossed and
smiling, looking like she's really enjoying every minute of this,
even though she's probably bored out of her tree.

"This is from your father and me." Meemaw hands me the
gift.

I rip off the paper and take the lid off the box. Inside wrapped
in pink tissue paper are four pairs of white ankle socks and a
cherry red Phillies T-shirt. I hold the shirt up to my chest. "Oh,
thank you," I blubber because I really do love it.

"We noticed your other one was pretty worn out," Pop says
with a smile.

"That shirt sure is bright red," Captain Ar says. "It goes quite
well with your blonde hair."

"Thank you," I say while I feel my cheeks burn fire hot. I
figure they're as red as my new shirt.

Meemaw hands me another gift with an envelope taped to it.
The gift is about six inches square and wrapped in paper designed
with little cartoon girls in dumb pink dresses and holding opened

pink parasols. "This one is from your Aunt Alma. Open the card first."

I do as Meemaw says and read the card to myself. I take a quick glance at Captain Ar, who's still smiling with her arms crossed, looking like she's loving every minute of this torture I'm going through.

"Well, what does the card say?" Pop asks.

"Happy birthday to a wonderful niece," I say. I wonder if Mom finally wrote and told her I was a girl.

I rip off the paper and open the box. I lift out six delicate, white handkerchiefs with borders of frilly lace in different pastel colors. At least, it's not a stupid doll.

"Aren't they beautiful!" Meemaw says. We both know the hankies will become hers in no time flat.

Pop picks up the third gift, the size of a shoe box. It's wrapped in the neatest paper with pictures of pool balls and pool sticks on a green background. "Who could this be from?" he says with tongue in cheek as he glances at the woman. He hands me the gift.

"It's from me," Captain Ar says with a bigger smile. "I hope you like it."

I have to keep my mouth from dropping open. I just met this woman a few weeks ago, and she's giving me presents? Let's add another piece to the Arlene Masters puzzle that I'm trying to figure out.

This time, I very carefully unwrap the paper, trying to save it. I open the box, and there are two other gifts wrapped in the same paper. I pick up the smaller gift, a small square box that could hold an orange, gently remove the paper, and lift the lid. Inside is something I've wanted forever. My own chocolate-colored cue ball. Those babies aren't that easy to find, so I wonder where in a dog's wagging tail did she ever get it? My eyes almost pop out of their sockets as I pick it up and caress it like it's made of gold. "Wow! That is too cool," I say. "Thank you!"

"What is it?" Meemaw asks. Remember, she doesn't know about me and Pop and midnight pool. I think she's about to find out.

"It's a billiard cue ball," Pop says. "I'll explain it to you later."

I place the cue ball back in its little box like I'm laying down a raw egg. I pick up the second box, take off the paper, and open the lid. Inside is a white book with the words HOLY BIBLE on the cover. I don't quite know what to make of this gift. I know the Bible is a book people read in church. Other than that, I don't know diddly squat about it. I carefully lift it from its box and shoot out a fake smile at her. "Ah-h, thank you, Captain Ar."

"Pockets," she says, "I pray that in time you'll come to love that book and all the wonderful words in it. It's the Guiding Light in my life, and it will be to you, too, if you read it."

Meemaw raises her index finger and says, "I know Marnie Fetterolf, our neighbor three houses down. She's a faithful church-goer. She often tells me she doesn't know what she'd do without the Good Book and the Lord in her life."

"I agree with that," Captain Ar says. "God is good to all of us through all circumstances of life."

Pop acts like he's not listening to the conversation as he gives me the last mysterious box. He handles it like it's made of delicate glass. "Pockets, this package was delivered from Chuck's Pet Store about an hour ago. The delivery man told me it came from your mother. It looks like you might be getting some kind of pet for your birthday." He studies the box with his super-suspicious eye.

"It better not be anything furry," Meemaw says. "She knows I'm allergic to all kinds of animal hair."

I gently set the box on the table. "How do we open it?"

"I think you're going to have to get a knife and very carefully cut along the edges on the top," Captain Ar says. "I don't see any rip-off tabs to make it easy to open."

I study the box with my nerves jumping up and down all through my body. I've never had any kind of pet in my life, not even a frog from the back yard. Next to the address label on the box there's a white sticker with the words LIVE ANIMAL INSIDE. HANDLE WITH CARE.

Meemaw hurries to the utensil drawer and brings back her sharpest paring knife. "Be careful with that," she orders.

"Very careful." Pop stations his hands firmly on both sides of the box. "Let me steady the box while you slice away."

I edge the blade into the box and start slicing a couple millimeters at a time, my nerves jumping out of their skin. In a few minutes, I have enough of the box opened to peek inside while Pop still holds the box.

"Yikes!" I yell and jump away from the box.

"What is it?" Captain Ar asks.

CHAPTER SIX

"It's-it's a baby alligator!" I say. "Or maybe it's a crocodile!"

"It can't be!" Meemaw says. "Who in their right mind would buy anyone an alligator? Your mother must have lost her mind."

Pop bends down and peeks into the box. "Pockets, it is an alligator. What are we gonna do with an alligator? They can grow to be over twelve feet long." Pop stands erect and scratches his head. Your mother has lost her noodle this time. What was she thinking?"

"Maybe it's a mistake," Captain Ar says.

Pop heads to the one lower cupboard near the stove. "No, on second thought, Nancy meant it. She did it just as a joke. But I don't think it's a bit funny." He opens the cupboard door, pulls out a large roast pan, and brings it to the table. "Let's get him into something more comfortable." He picks up the box and gently tilts it inside the pan until the alligator crawls out of his box.

I study the poor thing. He's about eight inches long.

"I have no idea what baby alligators eat," Pop says. "Pockets, go outside and bring in a couple hands full of grass. At least we can give him a nice bed. And we'll put something in there, maybe a jar lid with some water for him."

"Do alligators drink out of something like that?" I ask.

"Who knows?" Meemaw's tone is oozing with utter disgust. I'm calling your mother when she's off her shift and telling her to get over here and take that thing back to the store. We are not keeping an alligator!"

I glance at the clock on the wall above the sink. "But the store's not open now."

"She better get her tail over here first thing tomorrow morning and return it," Pop says. "If you're here when she comes, Pockets, you can go with her and either get some goldfish or a turtle or something small like that."

"I have a better idea," Meemaw says. "She can just give you the money instead. Then you can use it for whatever you'd like in any store."

The utter shock of such a gift from Mom rolls off me, and I almost find myself chuckling. "Let's call him 'Al'," I suggest.

"You better not name him," Captain Ar says. "They say when you name an animal, you can become attached to him immediately."

Of course, I know I can't keep an alligator in our house, and I'm sure Mom knows that, so I think she did it just to get Pop's goat. That thing had to have been shipped in from Florida. As often as I went in that pet store, I never saw any baby alligators.

I was too young to remember when Mom and Pop lived together, but Meemaw has told me they were always at one another's throat, pulling nasty practical jokes. One bad joke led to another until they finally split.

"You can call him anything you want," Meemaw says, "but he's going back to the pet store tomorrow."

"I know, I know," I say. "But, at least, when I'm grown up, I can remember I had Al the alligator for one day in my no-pet life." I shift my attention to Captain Ar, and she's got a look on her face that can mean only one thing: She's enjoying every minute of this fiasco, and I'm positive Al will be the topic of discussion at our next counseling session. I wish I had a million dollars. I could bet on that and know it's a sure win.

The very next morning, the start of another nice warm summer day, at nine o'clock sharp I park my bike in front of the Salvation Army post, ring the bell, and go in.

Captain Ar, dressed to kill in her starched uniform, is standing in her office doorway with a welcoming smile and beckons me to her office.

I go in, sit in "my" chair in front of her desk, and take off my cap. Yeah, I know I don't need to take my hat off because I'm of the female persuasion—the same as the woman. But I got into the habit the first time I met her, and now I'm stuck with it. I guess she does deserve some respect because she's so old. And, besides, anyone who knows what a chocolate-colored cue ball is can't be all that bad.

"Good morning, Pockets," she says with that warm smile, and her blue eyes penetrate my soul.

"Hi," I say and almost smile back, but I catch myself. I'm almost anxious to get here, but I can't let her know that. Over the last few weeks, she's not really intruded into my life. She must have a file on me as thick as Webster's Dictionary with her hundreds of questions and my mostly yes-no answers. If this is what counseling is like, I can handle it. I glance to the door behind the desk, but, so far, I've not been invited to the Friday Fun Nights nor to shoot pool, and I'm still wondering what I have to do to earn those rights.

"Did Al find his way back to the pet store?" she asks, snapping my attention back to her.

I knew it! I knew Al would be the star on the woman's questionnaire. "I guess," I say, my stare focused on those blue eyes. "Meemaw told me that Mom came and picked him up at six o'clock before I was up. Mom said she had to get to work at Sally's Luncheonette by six thirty and that she'd take Al back to the pet store when it opened at nine. I hope he makes it. We didn't know what to feed him."

Captain Ar leans her elbows on her desk and rests her chin on her folded hands. "So ... I'm assuming your mother will give you the refund money?"

"Meemaw told me that's what Mom said, but I'm not holding my breath. Mom's not too reliable. Knowing her, she might mail me an iguana or a tarantula instead."

"How does that make you feel when she breaks her promises?"

"It hurts," I say. I'm actually surprised I said that because I've never admitted to anyone that Mom's hurt me a lot through my life.

"Pockets, I'm very pleased with the progress we've made so far. You've been cooperative and, I might say, you've had a pretty good attitude. Today's session is going to be a little different, because I want you to tell me how you feel about certain things in your life instead of just answering mostly yes-no questions. Okay?"

Whoa. I'm not sure where we're going with this, but it sounds dangerous. I clam up and look at the floor. I'm not spilling my guts to this woman, cue ball expert or not.

"Pockets ..."

My heart starts to race, and I stare at the floor a long time then finally look at her. I know I can't win the silence game.

"You know you were given a break and not sent to reform school. I'm here to help you. We'll tackle your problems together and find a solution for them with God's help. That's one reason I gave you that Bible. God's Word has the answer to every problem we have in life."

"Will I ever get to shoot pool here?" After I say that, I feel really stupid. What does that have to do with me solving my problems. And by the way, who said I have problems anyway? "What problems?" I say, like I don't have a clue.

The woman suppresses a chuckle while she flips open a humongous file. My file, I assume. "Let's see." She points to the file. "You're barely squeaking by in school, you have no friends, you've been disguising yourself as a boy to shoot pool at Joe's in the wee hours of the night, you are, excuse me, you were a member of the Thorns, a part of your life that your grandmother and father knew nothing about, and you hardly ever see your mother. If they aren't problems, what would you call them?" She leans back in her chair, crosses her arms, and stares at me, waiting.

I think this through for a few seconds then shrug. "Issues."

"Issues?" This time she laughs out loud. "Pockets, the first step in solving problems is realizing you have some and face them head on."

I just stare at her blue eyes.

"Let's talk a little about your mother. When's the last time you saw her?"

"Last month. She picked me up the last day of school, and we went downtown to Matucci's for pizza to celebrate me making it to the eighth grade."

"Does she know about the bad grades you have?"

"Yeah, I told her, but she always says she didn't do well in school either and wonders what the teachers have against us."

"When you are with her, do you talk about important things? Does she want to know how you're doing?"

I shrug again. "Most of the time she tells me all about her three jobs and all the bills she has to pay. I just sit and listen."

"When did she leave you and your dad?"

"When I was about four."

"And … how do you feel about your mom?"

"I hate her." Suddenly, my eyes flood with tears, and I look at the floor. Where did those tears come from? Pockets Leland never cries. "I didn't mean that. I love her."

"Pockets …"

I wipe my eyes on my sleeve and force myself to look at the woman.

She grabs a tissue from a box on her desk and hands the tissue to me. "Do you know it's possible to love someone and hate them at the same time?"

"No," I say and blow my nose.

"It's only natural for a child to love his or her mom and want that love returned. When that love isn't returned, that hurt can turn to hate. Is that what you're feeling?"

"Yeah, I guess," I say as I sniffle and blow my nose again.

"Honey, I think your mother does love you, but she's doing a pretty bad job of showing it. From what you've told me, I think she has so many problems in her own life, she's feeling very unloved herself. And it sounds like your grandmother and your dad have hard feelings about her. Do you ever do anything to reach out to your mom and show her that you do love her?"

Did this woman just call me "Honey?" I stare at the sunset picture on the wall and try to think back into my past. "Well, every year I used to send her a birthday card and tell her I loved her, but she never said anything about the cards, so I stopped."

"Do you ever remember your mom hugging you?"

"No."

"How about your grandma or dad? Do they ever show you any affection that way?"

"Nah. Dad always says his family wasn't the huggy-kissy kind, and Meemaw, well, she just shows she loves me by cooking for me and working hard to pay the bills."

"Do you think they love you?"

"Yeah, I'm pretty sure they do, even though we don't hug."

"Do they ever tell you they love you?"

"Once in a blue moon."

"Do you tell them you love them?"

I pause, think back into my past, and shrug. "Not that I can remember. But they know I love them."

"How do you think they know that?"

"Well, I help Meemaw around the house, and I help Pop win quarters."

"Always with a good attitude?"

"Well, always with Pop. I love shooting pool. You know that."

"May I ask you to try to do something?"

"What?"

"Until I see you again, think of a way you could show all of your family that you love them—including your mother."

"How can I do that when I never see Mom? She's always busy."

"Maybe she says that just as an excuse, thinking you don't want to be with her."

"I never thought of it that way." Now the woman's got me thinking.

She reaches for a black book on her desk and opens it. Could it be a Bible?

"Pockets, do you know anything about Jesus or the Bible?"

It is a Bible. "Not much. When I was real little, a neighbor took me to church once, and I really liked it. I remember that Sunday school class. We sang songs, heard a story about Jesus, colored a picture of him hugging a little kid, and got some candy, but that's all I remember. I was really, really little."

"Do you know why you only ever went one time with the neighbor?"

"Well, Meemaw has always worked a lot of overtime, and she couldn't get up early enough to get me ready to go. And Pop and I would be too tired to get up because we'd be shooting pool the night before."

"I see," she says as she flips some pages in the Bible. "And what do you know about Jesus?"

I think really deep, deeper than I have in a long time to try to remember what that Sunday school teacher said. "I think he's God?"

"That's right," she says, "and he's our Savior. In another session, I'd like to tell you more about him, but for now, I want you to listen to something from the Bible that might help you with your family, and in the long run, with other people as well. Remember, at your birthday party, I told you the Bible has words of wisdom for every situation in our lives."

I nod and look at her, pretending to be interested.

She reaches over the desk and hands me a small paper. "Pockets, I know you've probably never read the Bible at all, but I'd like you to try. I put the reference John chapter three, verses one to eighteen on that paper."

I glance at the piece of paper and shift back to her.

"The book of John is in the New Testament about three fourths of the way through the Bible. I'd like you to take the time to just read those few verses, and the next time we meet, we'll discuss them. Write on a paper the things you don't understand. Will you do that?"

I nod. "Yeah, sure."

"Now, I want to read something very important from the Bible. Listen to this verse from the book of First Peter, chapter four: 'And above all things have fervent charity among yourselves: for charity shall cover the multitude of sins.' Pockets, the word 'charity' there means love. What do you think the verse means when it says love will cover a multitude of sins."

"I don't have an inkling," I say and then yawn. Something tells me we're getting into counseling now. My gaze drifts to the picture on the wall of the towering snowy mountains. How I'd love to be there right now.

"Pockets, look at me!" Captain Ar says loud enough to make my nerves jump, and I immediately glue my attention on her. She adds, "It means if you have love in your heart for others, you can forgive them for hurting you. Does that make any sense to you?"

I shrug again. I've become an expert shrugger over the years. It always works well in school.

"Answer me, please."

"I guess it means I should be the one to try to show my love and not always be waiting for others to show me love. I guess that means I have a selfish attitude."

"You are exactly right, and I believe your teacher, Miss Williams, was absolutely right when she told you if you'd apply yourself, you'd be an A student. You have a good head on your shoulders, Pockets, and I think you and I are going to help wake your Rip Van Winkle brain out of its long sleep. What do you say?"

What could I say? "Okay. And when can I shoot pool back there?" I point to the door behind her. Yep, I did it again. Another stupid question.

She closes the Bible and smiles at me. "Next time, I'll tell you how you earn the right to go back there. Until I see you again,

I want you to spend a lot of time thinking about what we've discussed today. Do I have your promise that you'll do that?"

"Sure," I say without one iota of truth to that word.

The woman closes our session in a prayer, and I'm outta there before she hardly can say goodbye.

CHAPTER SEVEN

I slam the post door shut, then check the air temperature and my sky clock. Today it's very humid and sticky. The air you can wear. I figure it's about eleven o'clock. I'm spazzed out. Did I just spend two hours with that woman?

I grab my bike and take off for the Higher Ups Park. No one is around, so I park the bike at a picnic pavilion and sit at a table. A gentle but hot breeze is whooshing through the park, and I hear a bird chirping. Everything else is summer silent. As I sit there, my mind drifts back to what Captain Ar said about my family, especially Mom. Like the Hoover Dam bursting, hot tears flood my eyes, and I start bawling like I've never bawled in my life before. I could give the Schuylkill River at flood stage a run for its money. I bury my head in my arms on the table and sob like there's no tomorrow. Why won't Mom come home? Where is she when I need her? Where's Pop when I need him? I cry buckets and can't stop … until—

"Hey, Tommi Jo, are you okay?"

My nerves almost jump me off the seat. I quickly try to wipe the tears away and pivot toward the voice.

It's Leona Kaminski!

"O-oh, h-hi," I stutter, looking for a hole to crawl into. No one, and I mean no one except the woman earlier today, has ever seen me cry. Why does it have to be Leona here? Now?

She sits down and looks at me like I have two heads. "Are you okay? Did your mom die or something? I've never seen you bawl before."

"Nah. I'm just dealing with some issues."

"Issues? I can identify with that. I've got issues too."

"You? You have issues? But you're one of the most popular girls in school!"

"It's nice to be popular, but it doesn't always take care of the loneliness I feel when no one's around."

"You feel alone sometimes?"

"Yeah. My parents are both so busy with their jobs, and my two older brothers are into sports big time, so we hardly ever eat supper together or anything like that." Leona sifts her fingers through her gorgeous wavy black hair and sighs. "I've already said too much, but I just want you to know I think I know how you feel."

I crack out a half-smile and wipe my eyes again. "Thanks," is all I can think to say.

Leona's gaze drifts toward the ball field. "I'm waiting for the guys to show up. We're going to play baseball later. Sometimes, I like to come here early when no one's around so I can just think."

"I do that a lot too," I say. "Today was a deep issues kind of thinking day. That's what turned the faucet on."

"Hey," she says as she takes a quick poke at my shoulder, "did you hear about Harry Garside, and Butch, and Charlie, and some other boys in town? They were arrested for vandalism and fighting over at the Eureka Park a few weeks ago. They were all sent to reform school, I think, for a year or something like that. From what I heard there were two gangs duking it out. I didn't even know we had gangs around here."

"Yeah, I had heard something about it." Did I ever.

"My cousin was arrested, too, and sent away."

"Who's your cousin?"

"Vince Ramsey."

Vince Ramsey? Runner? And I thought I had already hit rock bottom before Leona showed up. Now my tears have formed a puddle in the bottom of my heart. "He was in a gang?" I act totally dumbfounded.

"Yeah, go figure. Those guys have all kinds of secret lives. My family had no clue he was in a gang."

I wonder if they know he's a pool shark. I try to subtly wipe my eyes again and stand up. "Thanks for taking the time to talk to me. I gotta get going. My grandmother told me to be home for lunch. And I've got chores to do."

"Okay," she says as she stands. "See ya around."

"Yeah, see ya." I grab my bike and take off. All the way home, the floodgates open up again, and tears stream down my face.

Bawl baby. I've turned into nothing but a big bawl baby.

At home when I walk into the kitchen, I find a note on the table. Meemaw's not around, so I figure it's from her. The radio on the counter is blaring the noon news, but loud snores lead me to peek into the living room, where Pop's in a deep sleep. He didn't come home last night, so I figure he tied one on again. I go back to the table and pick up the note.

Tommi Jo,

I got called into work early today. Here's a list of things I'd like you to do. I have to work a double shift, so I won't see you until tomorrow.

Clean your bedroom and the bathroom.

Run the sweeper in the living room after your dad wakes up. He came in about 9:30 this morning and crashed on the sofa.

I have pork chops thawing out. At four o'clock, bake them with three potatoes for an hour and a half. I'll eat mine tomorrow when I come home. Keep an eye on the coal in the stove and how hot it gets. Remember, the last time you let it get too hot, and everything burned to a crisp.

If you want dessert, you can mix up some sugar cookies and bake them when the pork chops are done. You know where the recipes and all the ingredients are.

Thanks, Meemaw.

I take a deep breath and make big plans for the rest of my day. Instead of riding around town on my bike or reading my monthly Super Billiard magazine that Pop gave me last Christmas or doing crossword puzzles here at home, I have hours of work ahead of me on a hot, sticky summer day. What luck. My bedroom looks like a bomb exploded, and Meemaw says at my age I should be responsible, so she won't even venture in there for any reason.

"Your room's so dirty, someday I'll see the cockroaches carrying your bed away and with you in it," she always tells me, but we both know that's a big exaggeration. I've never seen a roach anywhere in our house. Ants and mice? Well, yes, but not cockroaches.

First, I quick make myself a summer baloney sandwich, gobble it down with some lemonade, and head upstairs with the Hoover vacuum cleaner, dust rags, and an old burlap bag I found on the back porch. The first thing I do is attack my closet and fill the bag with some old clothes I grew out of probably ten years ago, three pairs of worn-out holey shoes and good-for-nothing rubber boots, and three ancient coloring books with every page colored in them.

Next, I scoop out the junk under my bed. What a disaster! Mingled with zillions of dust bunnies are five different socks, two crossword puzzle books I thought walked away on me last year, four school assignments I was sure I had done but couldn't find, and my seventh grade arithmetic book! So that's where that rascal was hiding. Way back in the corner, I pull out a crumbled-up piece of paper and smooth it out. It's a stupid love letter I wrote to Runner after I first met him. I knew I'd never give it to him, but it was nice to dream. Wow, am I glad Meemaw never found this piece of literature, or she would have bombarded me with a zillion questions.

I sit on the bed, and when I glance at my nightstand, I notice the Bible that Captain Ar gave me peeking out from under a pile of magazines. Out of my jeans pocket, I pull the piece of paper she gave me and stare at it. I take out the Bible and lay it and the paper on my bed and decide to look the verses up after I've done all my chores. After all, I have until Friday to get that done.

I finish cleaning my bedroom and do the bathroom next. The whole time I slave away, I'm thinking about Captain Ar and our "discussion" this morning and my encounter with Leona Kaminski, wondering if there's one chance in a million we'll ever become friends. Or if I could become "friends" with her cousin. My mind and heart spend a lot of time on Runner, wondering where he is and for how long.

By late afternoon, the house, especially the upstairs, has become a sauna. Of course, we can't afford any air conditioners, so as if I'm not sweating like a pig enough, I carry the Hoover downstairs and get ready to run it in the living room, but only if Pop's awake.

"Pockets?" Pop says from the kitchen.

"Yeah, Pop?" I head to the kitchen and see him sitting at the table with a cup of coffee, his shaky hands massaging his temples. A lit cigarette is resting in an ashtray on the table. Pop looks like he was run over by a truck.

"I have a splitting headache," he groans. "I need to eat something. Will you make me a sandwich?"

"Meemaw wants me to make pork chops and potatoes for supper, Pop." I glance at the clock. "It's almost four. She told me to get them started now."

Pop slowly shakes his head. "Oh, Pockets, I can't wait that long. I need something to eat now."

"Okay, Pop." I walk to the refrigerator and pull out the baloney, butter, mustard, and a wrapped-up plastic bag with a handful of slices of bread in it. "I'll make you a sandwich." I lay everything on the table and get a knife from the utility drawer.

Pop holds up his half-full cup. "And fill this up for me, will ya?"

"Sure, Pop." While he massages his temples, I fill his cup, then slap a sandwich together for him quicker than he can say baloney. "Pop, are you going to feel good enough for us to shoot pool tonight? Meemaw's doing a double shift and won't be home until tomorrow."

"Yeah, I vaguely remember her telling me that this morning before she left." He gulps down almost the entire cup of coffee and relaxes back into his chair. "I think we'll be able to shoot tonight. We need those quarters. I'll just sleep off this miserable headache for a while. Maybe by eight or nine o'clock, I'll be in good shape. By the way, I did tell her about our pool escapades, and she didn't seem to mind at all. I think the quarters we bring home won her over."

"That's great, Pop." I hand him his sandwich and put the leftover sandwich stuff back in the fridge. "It'll probably take most of the day for me to get everything done around here anyway. Can you wait a few minutes now before going back into the living room? I have to run the sweeper in there quick. Then I'll get the supper going."

"Sure," he says and takes a bite of the sandwich. "It'll take me a while to eat this. It's too hot to eat anything, but I have to get something in my stomach, or I won't be good for nothing later on."

"It's been a while since we went to Joe's, Pop. I can't wait." I head toward the living room.

"You're a good kid, Pockets. You're a good kid."

"Eight ball in the side pocket." I take my shot and ace it. Another win for Pop and me. I play with my spankin' new chocolate cue ball, and the guys go bonkers over it. Most of them have never seen one. And, boy, can that baby move!

I glance at the clock—eleven forty. In a little more than two hours, we've won all the marbles and enough quarters to buy our groceries for the week. I tug my cap down a little tighter to make sure no renegade blonde strands slip out.

A late afternoon thunderstorm had blown through Ashland, capturing that hot, sticky air and escorting it out of town. I am absolutely thrilled about that. When I sweat like a pig, I always worry about my hair squiggling out from under my hat. And the cooler air in Joe's back room makes it easier for me to see without the cloud of cigarette and cigar smoke hovering over the table.

The whole time I'm shooting, I'm thinking about Runner … and missing him. Then he becomes the topic of conversation.

Jake Dombroski, down in defeat again, spews out, "If I hadn't hurt my finger at work today, you two would have been dead meat."

"Ah, Jake," Joe says, "you always have excuses. The Lelands are better than you and Lou. Why don't you just admit it."

"Just quit yappin' and rack 'em up again," Lou says as he chalks up his stick. "There's got to be somebody here who can send them home with their tails between their legs. Jake, let's make it us."

Jake pokes back his Pittsburgh Pirates ball cap and chalks up. "If Runner was here—"

"But he's not," one of the men in the side chairs yells out. "And I heard he won't be for months, maybe a year."

I hear that about Runner as I'm shooting, and my heart splits in two. I miscue, and the cue ball flies into a corner pocket. "Sorry, Pop."

"No worry," he says. "I'll clear the table on the next shot."

Joe relaxes on his referee chair in the corner and chews on his cigar. "I heard that Runner was in one of those gangs doing more than their share of mischief around town. I would have never guessed he was in one of those stupid gangs. They've done enough dirt around here. I'm glad the police finally caught two of the gangs and put them all away."

Not all of them, I feel like saying. Pop just gives me a look that can only mean "You are one lucky kid."

"Where are most of the gang members from?" Lou asks while Jake takes his shot and misses.

"I heard that one of the gangs was from uptown," Joe adds. "They were called the Thorns. Runner was in a gang called the Hawks. They're all locked up in reform school somewhere near Erie in northwest PA. Good riddance."

"The Hawks are all from the Heights in the south part of town," Jake says. "Charlie down at the foundry said as far as the police know, there were only three gangs in Ashland. Now that two have been busted up, the other one has free rein of the town."

"If the hoodlums learn their lesson while they're away, we should be done with gangs rumbling around here." Lou takes his shot, runs three balls off, then ends the game by shooting the eight ball in a corner pocket.

"Well, finally." Jake sweeps the quarters off the edge of the table. "Thanks, Pockets, for that miscue you had. That was real nice of you to do that for us so we could finish the game."

Pop unscrews his pool stick and puts it in its case. "We felt sorry for you," he says to Jake and Lou. "We thought we'd let you win one out of a dozen games, so you don't go cry babying home."

The men in the gallery join in with their own jeers and a round of laughter.

But I know exactly why we lost.

CHAPTER EIGHT

On Thursday evening at seven o'clock, me and Mom are sharing a pepperoni pizza at Matucci's. She's drinking a glass of lemonade, and I have an eight-cent bottle of Coke. She stopped at the house right after her shift ended and surprised me. She said we had some things to discuss. I'm wondering if Meemaw told her about my antics with the Thorns and me being in counseling. Or maybe she's going to pay me off for my birthday since Al went back to his swamp.

I'm taking Captain Ar's advice and cooking up a way to tell Mom I love her. But I'm nervous. I've never told anyone face-to-face that I love them.

We're sitting in one of the cushioned booths that are along three of the red-brick façade walls. Eight tables, five of them busy, fill the center of the room. The walls are decorated with mining tools like picks, lanterns, and helmets intermingled with pictures of days gone by. Mounted pictures show Ashland in its heyday with miners in all their gear, entrances to local mines that are all boarded up now, and even some carts being pulled by ponies.

The place is buzzing with almost all the booths full, two waitresses trying to keep up with the orders, and a juke box blaring Johnny Cash singing "I Walk the Line." As one of the few places in town with air conditioning, the cigarette smoke is minimal, siphoned out by some kind of neat fan system.

While I work on some pizza, Mom lights up a cigarette and rambles on between puffs and bites of pizza. I have no clue how smoke and pepperoni could ever taste good together.

"Tommi Jo," she manages to say between the pizza and cigarette, "your grandmother told me you were almost in a big pile of trouble because you were running with a gang. Where's your head, girl? A gang? The grades you're getting in school are bad enough, but a gang?"

Yep. I was right. Meemaw spilled the beans. "I know it was a dumb thing to do," I confess, "but it's over now, and I'm keeping my nose clean. Captain Ar is helping me do that. And … and there's something I've been wanting to tell you—"

"Who's Captain Ar?" She blows out a smoke ring, smashes her cigarette in an ashtray, and takes a bite of pizza.

"Oh, that's Arlene Masters at the Salvation Army. She's my counselor. I see her twice a week and—"

"That's good, Tommi Jo. I'm sure she'll help you keep out of trouble."

"Yeah, and she's been telling me—"

"I need to tell you something, Tommi Jo." Mom lights up another cigarette and takes a puff.

"Is it about your jobs, Mom? How are they going for you?"

"Not bad. Oh, that reminds me." She grabs her purse, yanks out a twenty-dollar bill and hands it to me. "Here, kid. Happy birthday. You can buy whatever you like with it."

"Wow, twenty whole dollars! Thanks, Mom." I shove the money in my jeans pocket. "And I'd like to tell you that—"

"The reason I wanted to see you is to tell you something." She rests her lit cigarette in the ashtray and looks me square in the eyes. She's never done that before.

"You're not sick or anything, are you, Mom?" I lose my appetite quicker than I could say pepperoni.

"No, it's nothing like that. Here's the deal. I'm moving to Kansas to live with your Aunt Alma. There's a brand-new candy factory opening out there in her hometown, and she said they pay real good. I'll only have one job instead of three, and I'll finally be able to get caught up on all my bills."

Now I feel like throwing up. "But, Mom, I'll never see you. Kansas is way out there in the middle of the country!"

"Oh, we can write and call each other. And I'd like you to come out and visit us. I'll pay your way. We'll keep in touch." She picks up her cigarette, takes a long drag, blows the smoke out, and crushes the butt in the ashtray.

"When … when are you leaving?" The faucet in my eyes is toying with my emotions.

"I gave my two-week notice at my jobs last week. I'm moving the first week of September."

"That's just a couple of weeks from now, Mom. What about all your stuff … and your apartment … and Meemaw … and me?"

"Tommi Jo, please try to understand." She reaches and gently caresses my hand. That's the first time I ever remember her touching me. "This is my big break. I gotta do this."

I feel a tear squirt out of my eye and trickle down my face. "Mom, I-I love you."

She squeezes my hand and gives me a half-smile. Her eyes get all watery. "This will all work out for the best, Tommi Jo. You'll see. And … I love you too."

Friday morning, I'm sitting in front of Captain Ar, ready for my next "session."

I hardly slept last night, thinking about Mom leaving, so I'm wiped out and don't feel like sitting here for an hour-and-a-half.

It's raining today, so Pop drove me here and will be back for me at ten thirty. I'd rather be home sleeping, but I need to be here. I want to be here. Sometimes I confuse myself beyond common sense. I guess my family's right. I don't have any.

Captain Ar flips my file open and gives me her warm smile, her blue eyes sparkling. "Good morning, Pockets. How are you doing today?"

"I-I-" I can't get any words out, and I burst out crying. I can't believe it, but I'm bawling again. It's raining outside, and it's pouring in my heart. "M-Mom's ... mov-moving to Kansas, and ... and I'll probably never see her again." I lean on the woman's desk, bury my head in my crossed arms and sob like a big baby.

In seconds, I feel an arm wrap around my shoulders. "I am so sorry, Pockets." Captain Ar gives me a warm embrace, something I've never felt before from anyone. I suddenly feel a kind of love from the woman that makes me feel like I'm really wanted. She gives me a handful of tissues and says nothing while I snort and blow my nose.

Finally, my eye faucets turn off, I pull myself together and sit up straight. I look at Captain Ar kneeling beside me. She releases her hug and stands. "There's always light at the end of every dark tunnel," she says with watery eyes and a smile. "Pockets, this will work out. You'll see." She pats my shoulder and walks behind her desk and sits. She hands me another wad of tissues because the ones she already gave me are nothing but a soggy little ball.

"Thanks," I say. I blow my nose and force out a smile.

For the next hour or so, the woman and I discuss some "issues." Oh, all right. They're problems—how Meemaw and Pop feel about Mom leaving, how I'm doing making any friends, how the pool games are going at Joe's, how I think I'll do in school this year. I find myself spilling my guts to Captain Ar like I've never done with anyone before. There's something about her. She cares. She really cares about me and wants to help me. I wish I had known her a long time ago. Then, I probably wouldn't have so many problems. If anyone would ask me if I have any friends, I'd have to admit that this woman is my friend.

Captain Ar has a short prayer, closes my file, and folds her hands on top of it. I've learned that means my session is officially over.

I stand, ready to check the waiting room to see if Pop has come for me yet.

"Pockets, have you ever heard of Ruth McGinnis?"

"No. Is she a kid who comes here?"

She chuckles. "No, she's a professional pool player. She's known as the 'Queen of Billiards.' She's from Honesdale, right here in our state. She's made quite a name for herself."

I sit down and fasten my undivided attention on Captain Ar. "I've never heard of Ruth McGinnis. Pop bought me a Billiard Magazine subscription last Christmas, but I've never seen anything in that about her. You mean she can shoot in poolrooms? How'd she learn to shoot? Did she disguise herself as a boy, like I do?"

Captain Ar shakes her head. "I'm afraid poolrooms, at least in this state, still don't openly welcome females. Ruth learned the game in her father's barbershop, where there were two pool tables for men to play on while waiting for a haircut. She started shooting when she was seven years old, just tall enough to reach the table, like you. She stood on a little stool to reach into the center of the table. Her father would give her a dollar every time she ran twenty or more balls straight."

"Wow. I wish Pop could pay me like that." I pause in deep thought then add, "So, I obviously am not going to be the first female champion pool player."

"It looks like Ruth beat you to it by a long shot, no pun intended. She's almost fifty years old and tours all over the country shooting in exhibitions. Her competitors are always men who have big heads before the games start. However, she beats every one of them easily and sends them packing with their tails between their legs."

I lean forward in my chair. "I would love to meet her sometime."

"I think that's possible."

"How?" My heart is doing the jig.

"On the last Saturday in September, she's going to be in Philadelphia at the Billiard Emporium, where an annual pocket billiard tournament is held. She'll be putting on an exhibition before the competition begins. And listen to this, Pockets. This year, for the first time, they're opening it up to females as long as they're sponsored by a male. The prize money for your age bracket is a hundred dollars for first place and fifty dollars for second. How would you like to enter the competition?"

I almost jump out of my seat and yell, "Would I?" I contain myself then ask, "How do you know so much about pool?"

"Oh, I like to follow women who are making a mark in history. I think Ruth McGinnis is making a great impact on billiards and the acceptance of women in the sport."

"What do I have to do to get in that competition?"

The woman smiles right up to her eyes. "I kind of thought you'd be interested. First and foremost, you continue at home to be a 'good girl' and help your grandmother and dad. Next, and listen carefully, school's starting in a few weeks. There will be no more failing grades, or I won't be taking you to the billiard competition." She looks at me, waiting for a response.

I scrunch up my face and sigh, "Oh, all right." This woman is a schemer.

She holds up a folded piece of paper. "You do your part, and I'll take care of getting you registered. I'll cover the registration fee. It's only fifteen dollars. I've already checked with your dad, and he said yes. He'll be your sponsor."

I raise my eyebrows and can hardly believe what I've just heard the last few minutes. "Oh, thank you." I hear the outer door shutting and assume Pop's here for me, so I stand to leave.

"Pockets, just a minute. One more thing."

I sit again and stare at her.

"I'd like you to come to the Friday Fun Night here tonight. It's time for you to meet some of the other kids who come for counseling."

I almost jump out of my seat again. "Will I get to shoot pool?"

"Did you read the Bible verses I asked you to read?"

My heart drops like an anchor to the bottom of my feet. I get ready to tell a whopper, but I can't lie to this woman. "Oh, I forgot."

The woman shakes her head. "No shooting pool tonight, honey. However, since you started counseling, you've been very cooperative, so I'm still inviting you to come tonight. Maybe next time, you'll get to shoot. The kids come from seven to nine."

Full of apologies for getting me fifteen minutes late to the Friday Fun Night, Pop drops me off and says he'll be back at nine. Even though it has stopped raining and the August air is toasty, Pop says he doesn't want me riding my bike home in the dark. The man has no idea how many times I've done that over the years when he was off on one of his binges and Meemaw was working. And my running with the Thorns at midnight? Come on, Pop! Where were you then?

As Pop drives away to who-knows-where, I hurry to the post, ring the doorbell, and go in. The waiting room is empty, but I hear a happy commotion, including smacking pool balls, coming from the back room. On the door leading to the woman's office, I see a sign tacked up that reads: "JUST COME THROUGH MY OFFICE TO THE ROOM IN THE BACK. Signed, Captain Ar."

I walk through the woman's office and into the back room, probably four times larger than the waiting room, and my eyes just about bulge out of my head. I see about a dozen kids playing all kinds of games. Two are playing ping-pong at a table in the center of the large room.

I immediately shift my attention to the well-used pool table, also in the center of the room. Two boys and one girl are holding cue sticks and standing around the table, and a fourth girl misses the cue ball by a mile and giggles. On the right side of the room are three boys shooting darts at a dartboard with a bright red and yellow target on it. I recognize Dale Montgomery from my class. We call him "Coochie." I wonder what got him in this exclusive club. I think I recognize one of the other boys who's a grade ahead of me, but I don't know his name.

To my left along the wall are three card tables with two metal folding chairs each. One table has a chess board, one has a Scrabble game, and the third one all the way in the back has a Monopoly board. Two girls are engrossed in that game.

Wait! Is one of those girls Leona Kaminski? It can't be.

It is. She said she had "issues," but what could Cinderella have ever done to be part of Captain Ar's army?

My gaze drifts to the back of the room hosting a kitchenette with a counter loaded with sodas, chips, cupcakes, and pretzels. Captain Ar, in her uniform of course, is there arranging the food. Helping her is a chubby man with white, wavy hair and a real neat short beard—an ancient man probably in his fifties and in his Salvation Army uniform. Captain Ar spots me and rushes through the noise and crowd toward me.

"Hello, Pockets!" She gives me a hug, and I kind of, awkwardly, hug her back. She smells wonderful, like real expensive perfume that I know she couldn't afford. I wonder what it is.

"I'm so glad you made it," she says. "I was concerned something had happened to you. I knew you had your heart set on being here."

"Pop came home late from wherever he was." I study every bit of the action in the room. "This place is pretty cool."

She turns and stands beside me as we face everyone. "Do you see anyone you know?"

"Yeah." I point in the dartboard's direction. "I know Coochie, ah, Dale Montgomery. He's in my class."

"Anyone else?"

I point to the back left corner. "Yeah, and this almost shocked the socks off me. Leona Kaminski is here. I always thought she had everything together in her life. She's one of the most popular girls in my class."

"You never know what's in the heart of anyone who's smiling at you."

"I don't know the other kids."

"There are three different area schools represented here. You'll get to know them if you keep coming on Friday evenings. And you might even form some friendships here with these kids." Captain Ar turns her attention to the group, claps her hands, and says, "Attention, everyone."

All the kids stop dead in their tracks and look my way. I feel like crawling under the ping-pong table. I can feel my face heating up big time. I tug my ball cap down firmer and cross my arms. Talk about embarrassing!

"For you who don't know this gal, this is Tommi Jo Leland," Captain Ar proclaims. "She prefers you to call her Pockets. Please welcome her."

"Hi, Pockets!" Everyone yells almost in unison as a round of applause fills the room.

"Now," Captain Ar says, "we're going to have our refreshments. Then you can get back to your games afterward." She points to the man at the counter. "Bill, would you please offer the blessing."

I watch as everyone bows their heads, so I do too. Bill prays, and we help ourselves to the snacks. Coochie and Leona make a point to small talk with me, but sadly, with no news about Runner. In about a half hour, the games begin again.

I mosey my way toward the pool table with a few others, and I get the biggest surprise of my life.

CHAPTER NINE

While Bill and Captain Ar clean up the food mess, everyone is busy having fun, although the pool table now sits idle. Leona invites me to join her while she and another girl, Trudy, continue their Monopoly game. But Coochie makes an announcement that draws me and Leona away from her game.

"Hey, Captain Ar, how about you and a partner take on Leona and me in a game of eight ball." He grabs a cue stick from the wall bracket. "I feel real lucky tonight."

Coochie's one of the dreamiest boys in my class. His wavy blond hair hangs over his forehead just far enough to rendezvous with his dark, brown eyes to put him in the running for Prince Charming of the eighth grade. He and Leona make a good pair. But I never knew she could shoot. And I wonder how good he is? And Leona too. I'll soon find out.

"I should help clean up the kitchenette," Captain Ar says.

I'm thinking the woman probably doesn't want to be embarrassed in front of me since she's become the big shot in my life for the last few months.

"No, go ahead," Bill says to her. "You've worked hard enough today. Have some fun."

"How about you, Pockets?" Leona grabs a stick, then runs her fingers through her hair. "Do you shoot pool? I'm not very good, but I'm learning since I've come here." She picks up a piece of chalk and scrapes it across her cue tip.

My heart just about leaps out of my throat and jumps onto the pool table. Would I ever love to shoot pool and show my stuff. Then I remember … aw nuts! I look at Captain Ar, and she subtly shakes her head.

"Ah … maybe next time," I groan and back away from the table to watch. Talk about mental torture! I decide to study who's the best pool player in the crowd and how I can wipe them out the next time I come. I flop into a chair along the wall, cross my arms, and wait for the fiasco to start.

The woman turns toward four boys throwing darts. "Reuben," she singles out one of the boys. "Would you like to be my partner in a pool match? Maybe you can help me win for once."

The room rumbles with a round of chuckles.

"Sure," Reuben says. He's a big guy, the football lineman type, with curly brown hair. His skintight T-shirt and shorts reveal mega muscles. He's got to be a high school football player, maybe from another school. I've never seen him before. Of course, I don't know any of Ashland's high schoolers either. When I've gone to football games, I never paid attention to any of the players. Who can see what they look like with those helmets on anyway?

Reuben grabs two sticks and hands one to Captain Ar. "We'll just see who'll come out on top tonight. Should we have mercy on them?" he says to the woman.

"Do you think they deserve it?" Captain Ar asks with a smirk. "They seem pretty cocky to me." She grabs some chalk and rubs the cue tip.

"Tell you what," Coochie says to Reuben and Captain Ar. "We'll have mercy on you tonight. You can even break them. I can feel it in my bones. This might be our night to shine." He and Leona throw smiles at each other.

I figure this should be a good one. These kids are setting the woman up for dynamite embarrassment.

"All right," Reuben says. "If that's the way you want it. You must want the game to end really quick if you want us to go first."

Ah, so he must be the pool shark of the bunch!

Reuben chalks up his stick, but then backs away from the table. "Captain Ar, why don't you break 'em."

"Are you sure?" she says, casually walking to the head of the table. While Coochie racks the fifteen balls, she places the cue ball on the right side of the table and gets into position to shoot.

She takes aim in perfect form and whack! She slams that cue ball into the rack so hard, two balls fly into corner pockets and one ball darts into a side pocket. The two balls she makes are solid colors, a blue two and a green six. The third one she knocks in is striped, a red and white eleven ball.

You have got to be kidding me! Tonight must be the night to have my socks knocked off more than once. This woman can shoot pool and how. No wonder she knows what a chocolate cue ball is and all about Ruth McGinnis. Guess who really got set up for embarrassment. Me.

"We'll take the low balls," Captain Ar says and continues shooting, running off four more solid-colored balls. She has a clear shot of her seventh and eight ball, which would win the game, but she misses her shot. I think it's a deliberate miss.

"Nice shooting, Captain Ar." Reuben stands by with a wide grin on his face. "Okay, hot shot Cooch. You better make your shot good. You won't get another chance."

I catch my mouth hanging open and clamp it shut. I am in total awe of Captain Ar!

She looks at me with a wink and that signature smile with her blue eyes flashing. She knows she got me good.

I smile back. I have to restrain myself from laughing out loud. Nobody would understand what that would be all about.

Coochie makes two balls then misses. Reuben finishes game one, and while the teams play two more games, Captain Ar shows her stuff. I sit there staring at her, wondering how she learned to shoot pool, wondering what she's doing wearing a starched uniform in a two-bit Salvation Army post in a run-down coal town in Pennsylvania, wondering why she's so different from anyone I've ever met. Just wondering.

For the first time in my life I've come to respect someone enough to listen to what they have to say. I can tell that all the kids respect her, and from the looks of some of them, they haven't respected anyone ever from the day they said "da-da" as impossible brats. Yeah, I can't help it. I respect her.

Is respect a form of love?

On Tuesday morning, after three do-nothing days just helping out at home, reading my billiard magazines and the Bible verses I finally remembered to do, working puzzles, and buzzing around town on my bike, I'm sitting in Captain Ar's office. I couldn't wait to get here. I gotta find out where she learned to shoot pool. I just gotta know more about her.

"Good morning, Pockets," she says in her usual bubbly manner.

."What makes you tick?" I'm real good at stupid questions. There's no messin' around with me when I'm curious about something. I just blurt out whatever pops into my head. Maybe that's why I don't have any friends.

The woman breaks into a smile that goes way beyond her eyes, and her eyebrows peak. "Excuse me?"

"What makes you tick? And where did you learn to shoot pool like that? Why do you care so much about kids? Why are you always so happy, and well, why are you the way you are?"

"My, my, aren't we full of questions today!" She opens a file and picks up a pen. "Shouldn't I be the one asking questions?"

"I just think it's cool that you can shoot pool, that's all."

"Well, thank you for the compliment, Pockets." She lays down the pen and relaxes into her chair. "Tell you what. You've been honest answering all the questions I've asked you, so how about if I answer your questions and in the order you asked them."

I feel like I'm about to hear some things that not many people know about this woman. I refrain myself from moving to the edge of my seat, but I get ready to just gobble up every word she says.

"First of all," she says with a smile, "I learned to shoot pool right here. I've already mentioned to you that I've been working in this office for twelve years. I'm not busy every single hour of the day. So after I had a few lessons from some of the kids who knew how to shoot, I just started practicing. It does take a lot of practice to master the game of pool, doesn't it?"

"Yep, but you're really good."

"Thank you. Next, you asked why I care about kids so much." She leans forward and whispers, "Pockets, can you keep a secret?"

I lean forward and whisper, "Sure. What is it?"

"I grew up in a home very similar to yours. In Pittsburgh. It was tough going until something changed my life, and we'll get to that in a minute." She relaxes back into her chair.

"Y-You grew up kind of like me? You're kidding."

"No, I'm not kidding. When I became an adult, I decided I wanted to help kids with problems, and God led me to serve here with the Salvation Army, and I love every minute of working with kids, with you."

I just nod and smile back at her. So, we have another day to knock my socks off.

She continues. "Then, I believe you asked why I'm so happy all the time."

"Right," I say.

"Jesus."

"What?"

Now her face practically glows. "I gave my heart to our Savior, Jesus Christ, many years ago. He changed my life and saved me from the disastrous downward spiral I was on. If I hadn't done that, I have no idea where I'd be today. I'd probably be in jail."

"You? In jail? No way."

"You have no idea the trouble I was getting in before I gave my heart to the Lord. Pockets, do you know that God loves you? When I came to understand the truth that he loves me, everything changed in the way I looked at things."

I sit and stare at her blue eyes, thinking back to that Sunday school class I went to so long ago. Yes, I remember the teacher saying something about God loving me and Jesus saving people. But I didn't understand what she meant. I don't really quite understand what Captain Ar means either.

"Pockets ...." She brings me back to the present. "Do you know what it means to 'be saved'?"

"No."

"Did you read the Bible passage I asked you to?"

"Yes."

"Did you understand it?"

"Not all of it. I got hung up on the verse that said something about being born again."

"Honey, being born again is just another way of saying you've been saved, or you've accepted Jesus into your life."

"Why would anyone need to do that?"

The woman reaches for her Bible and opens it. "Do you know what sin is?"

I shrug. We're really getting deep now. "I guess it's making mistakes. I never thought about it before."

"I'm going to read a few verses that are so very, very important. Remember when I gave you a Bible, and I told you it has the answers to all of life's questions?"

"Yeah."

"Well, the first question most folks want answered is what happens when we die. And along with that question, people want to know why we have to die. The Bible has that answer." She points to the book and reads, "'For all have sinned, and come short of the glory of God.' That verse is found in Romans. Pockets, when sin came into the world through Adam and Eve in the Garden of Eden, death came too. From that time on, we've needed a way to be free from sin, from death. That's where Jesus comes into the picture."

I just nod.

"I'm sure you've heard of heaven and hell, haven't you?"

"Yes. I remember that from the Sunday school class when I was a kid. Other than that and hearing hell as a curse word, I've never thought much about dying."

"Almost two thousand years ago, Jesus, the son of God, came to earth to die on a cross and take away the sins of anyone who believes in him. Anyone who does accept him as their Savior goes to heaven when they die. I know this is probably all new to you. But I've been praying about the right time to share my faith with you. Do you understand any of what I've told you?"

"A little."

She turns some pages in her Bible. "I want to share just one more verse with you. This verse changed my life. It's also found in the book of Romans. It says, 'That if thou shalt confess with thy mouth the Lord Jesus, and shalt believe in thine heart that God hath raised him from the dead, thou shalt be saved.' Pockets, one thing you need to understand is, that besides just making mistakes, and we all do, we sin. Sin is anything God considers wrong and an offense against him and his holy laws. In the heart of every person is a conscience. I'm sure you know when you've done wrong. Can you tell me what you think you might have done in your short life that you could call sin?"

Oh, brother, can I? My mind races back through time, and I feel like crawling under the woman's desk. I slouch down into my chair while I remember some pretty awful stunts I've pulled. No, not stunts. I guess they're sins.

"Pockets, do you have an answer for me? And please sit up straight."

I shoot up rigid in my chair, stare at her, and say, "Well …"

She doesn't move a muscle and stares back. We both know I'll soon be spilling my guts.

"Okay, okay. Here goes. I threw a rock through a neighbor's window and stole school supplies from the Woolworth store so I could be a member of the Thorns."

She just sits and waits.

"I've played hooky from school a lot. Last year, I missed about fifty days all year. I hate school. If you call getting lousy grades a sin, then I guess we can add that to the list too."

She crosses her arms and gives me an understanding smile. "Anything else?"

I feel like the woman's blue eyes are reading my mind, and she already knows me inside and out. "Sometimes I lose my temper at home and talk back to Meemaw and Pop. I've done my share of swearing over the years and telling whoppers too. I guess that's about it."

Captain Ar nods and purses her lips. "That's a good start, Pockets. Let me ask you a question."

"Yeah?"

"Do you think deceiving someone is a sin?"

Uh-oh. I think I know where we're going with this. "Yes, I suppose so."

"How about dressing like a boy to shoot pool at Joe's?"

I just look at the floor and say nothing.

"And how about sins of the heart?" she adds.

I look at her. "What are sins of the heart?"

"How's your attitude at home?"

"Not very good lots of times."

"Are you jealous of anyone?"

"Sometimes I wish I had everything together like the real popular kids in school. But I guess some of them really don't have it all together—like Leona."

"Remember when you told me you hated your mother? Do you think hate is a sin?"

"Well, yes, but I don't really hate her. You know that."

"Yes, I do know that, and I'm very thankful for your honesty."

I smile at the woman and melt back into my chair. I feel like I've been beat up.

She leans forward and folds her hands on top of my file. "I'll tell you what we'll do. We're going to wrap up your session for today, and I want you to do some deep thinking about all we discussed until I see you again." She picks up her pen and a paper and starts writing. "I want you to look up these verses we discussed today when you're at home and think about them. On Friday, we'll talk about them again, and I'll try to answer any questions you have. How does that sound to you?" She stops writing, folds the piece of paper in half, and hands it to me with the smile I've come to love.

"I'll try." I take the paper and stuff it in my jeans pocket.

"That's all I ask," she says, then closes with a prayer.

I stand and start toward the door.

"Pockets."

I turn and look at her.

"I love you, and I want the best for you. Remember that."

I just nod and scram out of there in three seconds flat.

I hightail it home, smiling the whole way, thinking about the woman telling me she loves me. I think back to the last time I saw Mom when she said she loved me, but somehow it doesn't seem like she meant it. But Captain Ar? Her words flew right into my heart and made me feel warm all over. It's nice to be wanted.

I park my bike next to the front porch and rush into the living room, then to the kitchen. Meemaw is there cooking up a storm with a list of chores for me to do. It's corn-on-the-cob season. Every year we buy five or six dozen from the farmer/huckster and cut the corn off the blanched cobs to freeze.

This year, Meemaw bought seven dozen at twenty cents a dozen, so the kitchen is already floating in corn. My job is to husk all the cobs in the back yard, which is a killer on a hot, sticky day. But I'm as happy as a puppy with his first toy that the August weather has cooled down, at least today. It's sunny, but the air is nice and crisp.

I study the mess in the kitchen and detect a bad attitude rumbling in my gut because I have to help. Then, I remember what I just heard from Captain Ar. I decide to wipe away my sour puss, replace it with a smile, and help Meemaw.

Sometimes I worry about her. She looks awful tired with all the hours she puts in at the factory. I wish Pop could get a steady job. That would really help. However, today I'm glad he's not working. I spot him sitting in the yard husking away. I say a quick "I'm home" to Meemaw and rush out into the yard to join in the "fun."

With only two quick breaks for a corn-on-the-cob lunch and ham-and-cheese sandwich supper, we finally finish the corn and clean up the kitchen, including me scrubbing the floor, by seven o'clock. We did fifty bags, and we're all glad Pop bought that secondhand chest freezer last month. Now it has some company.

All three of us are tired beyond words. Meemaw has already crashed into her chair in the living room and is half-sleeping, half-reading the newspaper, and Pop is sacked out on the sofa. I finish drying all the corn-mess dishes and utensils, crawl up the stairs to my bedroom, and flop on the bed cluttered with dirty clothes and smelly socks, three crossword puzzle books, and a pile of my billiard magazines. The latest edition just came in the mail yesterday, so I grab it from the top of the pile to dig in. I notice my Bible buried underneath the pile of magazines. I pause then remember the paper Captain Ar gave me.

I pull my Bible out from under the pile, retrieve the paper from my jeans pocket, and unfold it. The first reference she wrote is Romans 10:9. I haven't a clue where Romans is in the Bible, so I check the list of book titles in the front and see that Romans is near the back. I flip through the pages until I find the verse. "That if thou shalt confess with thy mouth the Lord Jesus, and shalt believe in thine heart that God hath raised him from the dead, thou shalt be saved." I look at her paper again and see another reference, Romans 6:23. I go back a few pages in the Bible and read "For the wages of sin is death; but the gift of God is eternal life through Jesus Christ our Lord."

I read the verses again and do some serious thinking as Captain Ar said I should do. I think about her and how different she is from anyone I've ever met, and she says it's because of Jesus. I think about sin and heaven and wonder if it's all true, or if we just die like a dog and that's all there is to it. Then I think about Jesus and him dying on a cross to take away my sins, and I don't quite understand. But deep down in my gut something's telling me it is all true. I wonder if Meemaw and Pop and Mom ever heard all this stuff about Jesus, and if they did, what they think of it. I start to read the verses again, but my heavy eyelids close and ...

CHAPTER TEN

R-R-Ring!

It's Thursday morning, and while I'm making Pop a breakfast of eggs and toast 'cause Meemaw's doing another double shift, I get a phone call I've been waiting for all my life.

I hurry to the phone mounted on the kitchen wall and answer, "Hello?"

"Hey, this is Leona. Do you wanna go bowling on Saturday?"

Even in the summer, my feet have been cold a lot lately because I'm always getting my socks knocked off of me. "Leona? Are you sure you have the right number?"

"Tommi? I mean, Pockets?"

"Yeah?"

"Sure, I have the right number. Are you doing anything Saturday afternoon?"

I quickly focus on my short future and hope that me and Pop will be shooting Saturday night, but what about that afternoon? That part of my busy schedule is blank. "Not that I can think of. Why? What's happening?"

"Well, Marylou, Pam, and I are going bowling, and I was wondering if you'd like to go with us? Mom's going to drive me to Sunset Lanes at one o'clock and come back for me in a couple of hours. We'll drive right by your house, and you can go with us."

I almost gasp out loud, and I'm sure if Leona could see my face, it's frozen in an utter shock mode. Me? Going bowling with three of the most popular girls in the eighth grade? I'm immediately suspicious of Leona, wondering what she's up to, but then it dawns on me. She's in Captain Ar's brigade, and Leona might really be trying to be my friend. "Ah-ah, yeah," I dribble out. "I think I can go."

"Super!" Leona says. "Mom and I will pick you up about ten minutes to one. Marylou and Pam will meet us at the bowling alley. You'll need about two dollars for the shoe rental and three games we plan to bowl. And bring extra money if you want to get something at their snack bar. I guess you know all that. I'm sure it's not the first time you've ever been at the bowling alley."

Little does she know it will be. "Sure. Thanks!"

"Super. See you Saturday. Bye."

"Bye." I hang up and smile like there's a million bucks in my pocket. She might even have some news about Runner. Maybe he's home!

But then, out of the blue, a thought suddenly hits me like a punch in the gut. I have never, ever been around Marylou Evans or Pam Mensch. They're cheerleaders, for Pete's sake. They'll never speak to lowlife like me. And I've never picked up a bowling ball. Are they setting me up for one of the most embarrassing episodes of my life?" My pure joy vanishes like a puff of Pop's cigarette smoke, and I sink into a pit of nasty thoughts.

Why in a pig's snout did I say yes?

I'm sitting in front of Captain Ar on Friday morning. I couldn't wait to get here and spill my guts to her. I have so much on my mind, we might be here until Christmas. We've already been solving the world's problems for almost an hour. Then I bring up Leona and the bowling invitation for the next day.

"Captain Ar, I've never been invited anywhere by any kids I know. I'm just wondering if I'm being set up for a big fat humiliating crash."

"I don't think you have to worry about that," she says. "Leona's been in counseling longer than you have, Pockets. She's come a long way, and I believe she's very sincere in trying to be your friend. She's realizing what's really important in life, and being a loyal friend to others is one of those important things."

"I was thinking of calling it off."

"I hope you don't do that. I'd like you to go with those gals and interact with them as best as you know how. Consider it part of the counseling you've received here. Would you do that, just for me?" She releases that warm "I love you" smile.

I think I'd jump off a cliff for this woman. "Yes, I'll go … but just for you."

"I believe you're going to be pleasantly surprised at the outcome. Leona's made tremendous strides in her time here. You probably think she could never be your friend, but that's not the case."

"I hope you're right," I say.

"I hope so too. And I'm wondering if you'll step out of your comfort zone another way."

"How's that?"

"What are you going to wear to go bowling?"

I pause then say, "I don't have a clue. Never gave it a thought."

"What do you think the girls will be wearing?"

"Oh, I know their type. They'll wear ironed-to-perfection, pullover shirts with collars and Bermuda shorts, bobby socks, and sneakers. They'll all have different colored shirts so they don't clash. And their long curls will fall perfectly over one eyebrow onto their shoulders."

"Do you have Bermuda shorts?"

"No, but I think I have tan pedal pushers. Meemaw bought them at a yard sale last summer, but I've never worn them. I feel at home in jeans."

"Well, give your outfit some thought. You want to feel as comfortable as possible, so may I suggest leaving that Phillies cap at home and let your beautiful blonde hair fall over one eyebrow onto your shoulders." She smiles and winks at me.

I nod and smile back.

She folds her hands on her desk and says, "Let's move on to another subject. Have you been reading those Bible verses I gave you?"

"Yes, ma'am. I've read those verses over and over, but I don't quite get them."

"What is it you don't understand?" Captain Ar grabs her Bible and opens it.

"If Jesus is God, why would he want to come to earth as a man and die? Why would God do that? And how could God die?"

"I know it's hard to understand. Jesus was a hundred percent man and a hundred percent God. When he shed his blood for us and died on the cross, the man Jesus died, but the "God" Jesus didn't die. That's why he was able to walk out of that tomb three days later. He conquered death for all who believe in him. That's what Easter is all about."

"But it's hard to understand why he'd want to die such a horrible death."

"Simply because he loves us and doesn't want us to have to pay the penalty for our sins," she says as she turns pages. "Listen to this. Romans chapter five, verse eight says, 'But God commendeth his love toward us, in that, while we were yet sinners, Christ died for us.' God has a love for us that we simply can't understand. We have to just accept it by faith, realize we have sinned against a holy God, and ask for his forgiveness. When we do that, we are saved from our sin, and we become a child of God."

I look down at the floor and think deep. Yeah, I've done some pretty rotten things. I'm a good candidate for the worst kid louse in Schuylkill County.

"Pockets."

I look up, and the woman's blue x-ray eyes are penetrating deep into my soul. I feel my eye faucets turn on, and tears well up not only in my eyes but in my heart.

"Have you come to the conclusion that you need a Savior?"

"I want to believe, but Meemaw told me one time I just had to be good to get to heaven."

"Have you been that good?"

I just shake my head.

"Has your father ever talked about God?"

"Only in swear words."

"There's not enough good we can do to outweigh the sins we've committed against a holy God. Do you understand that?"

"I think so."

"Have you come to the point in your life that you're sorry for your sin?"

"Yes."

"Well, would you like to ask Jesus Christ to save you?"

I think deep again as I stare at Captain Ar. She's so different because God changed her. I love her because she loves me. And God loves me too. "Yes, I'd like to ask Jesus to forgive me and change me so I can go to heaven."

"That's wonderful," she says. "What you need to do is so simple, some people think it's too simple. Just open up your heart to God and ask Jesus to come into your life and save you. But you must mean every word with your whole being. He'll make you a new person. The Bible tells us the Holy Spirit dwells inside everyone who becomes a born-again Christian. You are going to look at things a lot differently than you've ever seen them before."

I wipe away a tear that has leaked out of one eye. "I've never prayed in my whole life. How do I do that?"

"I'll help you." Captain Ar's smile lights up the whole room. "Just bow your head, close your eyes, and repeat after me the words I say. And I want you to mean every word."

"All right." I do as she says and listen.

"Dear Jesus ..." she says.

"Dear Jesus ..."

"I know I've done a lot of wrong things in my life and have sinned against you."

By now my eye faucets have opened like a busted dam. I wipe the tears away on my arm as I repeat the prayer.

"Please forgive me and save me so that I can go to heaven someday."

"Thank you, Jesus, for saving me, amen." I look at the woman, and tears are flooding her face. She dabs the tears with a tissue then hands me the tissue box.

"Y-You're bawling," I babble as I nurse my wet face.

"Pockets, honey, they're tears of joy. You've just made the most important decision you'll ever make in your life. Welcome to the family of God."

Tears of joy. I never knew there could be such a thing. I analyze the water streaming down my cheeks and decide my sad tears have turned to happy tears. For the first time ever, I feel like those tears are cleaning my heart of all its sadness and crud.

CHAPTER ELEVEN

It's Friday night, and Pop gets me to the post on time. I decide to leave my ball cap at home. As I'm hoping to shoot pool for the first time at the post, I've drawn my hair back into a ponytail.

I'm greeted with a hug by Captain Ar and join Leona, Coochie, and the rest of the kids all making small talk and already targeting their favorite games. Bill's back at his station in the kitchenette getting the snacks ready. No one has claimed the pool table yet, so I'm drooling as I wait to see if this is my big chance.

Captain Ar wraps her arm around my shoulders and whispers, "Should we take two guys on?"

"I can't wait," I whisper back.

"Go get a stick," she whispers. "The best one is all the way on the right side of the wall rack. Get that one before someone claims it." She walks to the pool table, slides out a cue stick case from under the table, pulls out the two halves of her stick from the case, and screws them together.

While I retrieve a stick from the wall rack, I hear her say to Coochie, who's already helping himself to some chips, "Cooch, how about you and Reuben taking Pockets and me on in a game of eight ball."

I'm almost certain nobody knows I can shoot.

"Sure, although you better be on tonight," Coochie says as he grabs a stick off the rack. "Reuben and I have been practicing."

"Pockets, can you shoot?" Reuben retrieves a stick and chalks up.

"A little," I say and chalk up. I throw a sarcastic smile at the woman.

She smiles back, goes to the table, and racks the balls. "Go ahead, Coochie. You guys can start."

"Okay," he says, then places the cue ball on the table. "You asked for it." He whacks the balls, making the striped purple and white twelve in a side pocket.

"Good job, Cooch," Reuben says with a cocky smile. "Now run off all the stripes, and don't even give them a shot."

Coochie chalks up, makes two more striped balls but then misses. The rest of the balls are spread all over the table, perfect for a solid-ball run. "Aw, phooey," he groans. "Go ahead, Captain Ar. It looks like we're goin' down fast."

"I'll let Pockets shoot first," she says as she stands back.

"Are you sure?" Reuben smiles at Coochie with that look that says, "Oh, is this ever gonna be a cinch."

"Yeah, are you sure?" I say to the woman with my own smirk.

"I'm sure," she says. "Go ahead."

"Wow," Coochie says, "you're really giving us a break, Captain Ar. Nothin' against you, Pockets."

"No problem," I say as I study the table and strategize my next few shots. I take a quick look at the woman, who is standing with her arms crossed and smiling to beat the band.

"Go get 'em," she says.

I shoot the yellow one ball and make two more solids with perfect position for the next shot. By this time, the room grows quiet. I look up and see everyone circling the table, watching my next move.

"Wow," Leona says. "I didn't know you could shoot like that."

"Hey," Coochie says, "I think we've been skunked."

"Yeah," Reuben says. "Pockets, what are you … some kind of kid pro?"

"Well, I—"

"She's just had the opportunity to shoot a lot," Captain Ar interjects. "She just might be a pro someday."

I take aim at the orange five ball next and whack! I make that ball plus the remaining three solids. The only one left is the eight ball, an easy shot. As I chalk up to shoot and end the game, Leona starts chanting, "Go, Pockets, go! Go, Pockets, go!"

In seconds, every kid in the room joins the chant. My glance shifts to Captain Ar, who is still standing with her arms crossed, her smile practically lighting up the room. She just nods, and I shift back to the table.

I take the shot, pocket the eight ball, and everyone erupts with applause and cheers.

"Pockets! Of course!" Coochie slaps his forehead. "How could we be so stupid? Who else would have the nickname Pockets but a pool shark!"

For the first time in my life, I feel like I'm finally "one of the gang," the good gang, and my heart practically bursts with a new kind of joy.

"Bye, Leona!" I say as I get out of her car late Saturday afternoon. I hurry into my house and blow out a sigh of awesome relief.

Captain Ar was right, as usual.

I took the woman's advice and wore my Phillies T-shirt, tan pedal pushers, and my hair down without my cap. Leona thought the T-shirt was "cute." She went far beyond what I ever expected from a girl of her status in her treatment of little ol' me.

She even bought me a hamburger and Coke, though I had the thirty-five cents to buy them myself.

As far as the other girls, they actually talked to me like I was a human being. They probably got lectured big time before we ever got there. Although I'd never bowled before, my one hundred and twenty average for three games almost matched the others, even though they're the "athletic" type. I blame all their gutter balls on the two teen hunks in the alley right next to us. The girls eyed them the whole time and giggled their way into their attention, which became the girls' entire focus for the afternoon.

The biggest "wow" time for me came when Leona told me Runner will be home in time for school. Exactly when? She didn't know. Since he's in ninth grade, I'll be lucky to see him once all year when passing him in a hall between classes, but I'm counting on seeing him at Joe's.

I live for that moment.

Saturday night. Nine o'clock. School's starting in ten days, the Tuesday after Labor Day, as usual. Me and Pop know my times of shooting with him will be skimpy, maybe only on Saturday nights, so we're at Joe's for an hour already on a hot winning streak.

For a nice change in her hard life, Meemaw's puttering around at home tonight instead of working overtime, so she knows what me and Pop are doing. She says she doesn't mind my pool escapades because those extra quarters really come in handy.

I've got my hair all tucked up under my ball cap, and I'm dressed to kill in my usual long-sleeved shirt and jeans. The same old gang is here, including Joe and griping Jake. Pop and I have already cleaned up four games, but for some reason, I feel weird at Joe's tonight, almost like I don't belong here.

Pop racks up the fifth game when the door opens, and in walks Runner.

The room erupts in a round of welcomes.

"Hey, Runner!" Joe says. "We're glad you're back!"

"Yeah," Jake says. "It's been boring around here without you. We need you big time. These Lelands have been brutal. I'm going broke!"

"Glad to be back!" Runner smiles as he opens up his cue case and screws his stick together. He's still the hunk he used to be, but he's put on more muscle. He's very tan and his brown curls, although pretty short, are slicked back accompanied by Elvis sideburns, which make him a super hunk. My heart races so fast it jumps up into my throat as I stare at him, wondering what he learned at reform school ... wondering if they had a pool table there. If not, he might really be off, and this will be my big chance to show him my stuff.

"C'mon, Runner," Jake says. "It's time to send the Lelands packing."

"I've been dreaming about this moment," Runner says as he walks to the table. "Although, Jake, you might not want me for your partner. I haven't touched a pool table in three months."

"We thought you were sent up for longer than that," Joe says.

"I kept my nose clean, so I got an early release," Runner says.

"Pop," I say, "this is our big chance!"

Pop slaps a quarter on the table railing then racks the balls. "How about a game of straight pool to a hundred. We'll even give you guys a head start. Go ahead, Jake. Break 'em."

"This is gonna be so good," one of the men says from the gallery, and everyone applauds and hoots. "I'll even throw in an extra quarter to the winner."

"Me too," another says.

"You break them," Runner says to Jake, and the game begins.

Jake makes two balls on the break then runs five more.

Pop goes next and runs the rest of the rack plus three more balls in the second rack.

Runner makes only two balls and misses. "I told you I'm rusty," he groans.

It's my turn. I park my racing heart along with the other weird feeling far back in my brain and really focus.

"C'mon, Pockets," Pop says. "Show them who's boss."

I run twenty-five balls in a row to a roomful of cheers.

For the next half hour, the game continues with Jake being red hot, making up for Runner's poor showing. The score is ninety for us and eighty-five for them.

Runner breaks a new rack and makes three balls. On his next shot, he miscues.

I'm next. Despite my crazy, rambling thoughts, I analyze the table and plan my strategy. I only need to run off ten balls, and we've got the game.

"Steady now," Pop says. "The table is an easy one."

I nod and chalk my cue.

Joe announces, "The score is Lelands ninety. Jake and Runner eighty-eight."

I'm on my game and have no trouble running the ten balls. The place erupts in applause and cheers as Pop scoops the quarters off the railing and stuffs them into his pocket.

Suddenly, like a light bulb going off in a pitch dark closet at midnight, some of Captain Ar's words pop up in my brain: "Do you think deceiving someone is a sin? How about dressing like a boy to shoot pool at Joe's?"

While the crowd goes bonkers over us winning, my brain focuses on the woman's words and shuts out all the noise. I finally realize why I feel so yucky about being here. I'm living a lie. But I have Jesus in my life now. How can I keep living a lie?

"Pop," I say to him over all the noise, "I can't do this anymore."

"What's wrong?"

"I can't pretend I'm a boy anymore!" I say and grab the visor of my cap.

"No, don't!" Pop reaches to try to stop me.

But I whip off my hat, and my hair falls to my shoulders.

In seconds, the room grows as silent as a summer breeze. My glance darts around the room, first at Runner, whose mouth is hanging open. Every face is masked with the same shocked look. Then everyone erupts in explosive laughs and louder applause.

"He's—she's a girl!" Jake says. "Now I really am humiliated!"

"But what a girl!" Runner says with a smile that tells me he's really impressed.

"Lucky Leland!" Joe's voice oozes with a strange mixture of sarcasm and anger. "You know the rules! No females allowed in this poolroom!" Then he bursts into laughter. "But ... Pockets is no ordinary female!"

"Yeah," one of the men in the gallery yells. "She's earned the right to be here anytime she wants."

Another one yells, "Any gal who can shoot like that deserves a life membership!"

"I'll have to think about that," Joe says.

I look at Pop, whose face is draped in a shroud of disappointment. He shakes his head and starts to walk away.

"I'm sorry, Pop," I say. "Really sorry."

CHAPTER TWELVE

Tuesday morning, me, Pop, and Meemaw are lined up on chairs in front of Captain Ar in her office. My nerves are dancing the jig because this is the first time all three of us have had a meeting with the woman. I have no clue what we'll be hashing over, but I'm hoping we can talk about the end of my shooting career at Joe's. Since Saturday night, Pop's hardly said boo to me. He's really ticked at my antics this time. But he just doesn't understand.

Captain Ar leans forward and folds her hands on her desk. "I've asked all of you here today to discuss Pockets' progress. As you know, her counseling ends this Friday." Her blue eyes smile at me.

Although I already know my time with this woman ends in a few days, when I hear those words, I feel like my heart is ripping to shreds. I don't want to leave.

Captain Ar continues. "Mona and Tom, over these last few months, have you seen any changes at all with Pockets at home?"

Pop just stares at the woman without saying a word. He looks like his thoughts are circling the moon.

"Oh, I've noticed quite a bit of improvement," Meemaw says, looking at me with her best eyelashes flashing then focusing back on the woman. "But she's really been a pretty good kid all along."

Talk about telling whoppers. I roll my eyes with tongue in cheek as Captain Ar and I exchange we-know-better smiles.

"How about you, Mr. Leland?" Captain Ar asks.

Pop's thoughts bring him back from wherever he was. "Well … I've noticed her attitude is much better doing chores, although like Mona said, Pockets has always been a pretty good kid. And since she's not running with those hoodlums, her bad language has cleaned up."

He should talk.

"She's been keeping her room much neater too," Meemaw adds. "The last few weeks it hasn't looked like a bomb exploded."

"So, what do you both think of the grades she's earned in school?" the woman asks.

"Oh, man," Pop says. "Now, there we definitely need a big change. She almost flunked last year."

"Not quite, Pop," I throw in. "I only had two F's. I needed three."

"I did say almost," he said sharply. "You've just gotta do better this year."

"Mr. Leland," Captain Ar says, "Pockets has told me you two often shoot pool at Joe's a few nights a week and quite often until after midnight. If she's going to school dead tired the mornings after, I can see why her grades are so bad."

Pop gives me a half-held-back disgusted look. "Well, it so happens that it will not be an issue any more. The boys at Joe's all know she's a girl since last Saturday night, and Joe's not sure he'll let her back in."

"That little bit of money they made really helped," Meemaw says, "but now that I see how much she's maturing into a young lady the last few months, I'd rather not see her hanging out at Joe's, even though she's told me how much shooting pool means to her."

Pop leans forward in his chair and raises his index finger. "I must admit she's growing into a young lady, and Joe's is probably not the place for her anymore. But she needs all the practice she can get if she's going to compete at the end of the month at that Billiard Emporium. We really could use the hundred-dollar prize money."

"I think I have the answer for all these issues," Captain Ar says. "Yes, Pockets' counseling does end on Friday, but that doesn't mean her time to come here must end. If she wants to continue to come to Friday Fun Nights, she's certainly welcome."

"You mean it?" I break into a smile that might just match hers. "Then I'll get to see Leona and Coochie and all the others." And you!

"Of course," she says. "I am so glad you're forming friendships with some of those kids. And every afternoon after school, if the office isn't busy with counseling, you may come and practice. The table gets pretty lonely in that back room all by itself. If I don't have a lot of paperwork, I'll challenge you and push you to your limits."

"Wow!" I say. "That will be so cool."

Pop relaxes into his chair and sighs. "Well, that'll solve the problem of her practicing. As far as me shooting at Joe's, there are a few pretty good shooters there, who I'm sure will love to team up with me."

"Like Runner?" I ask, although that was a stupid question because I'm not gonna be at Joe's anyway.

"H'm … maybe," Pop answers. "But that might not work. With Runner as my partner, we might not get any takers. We'd wipe out everybody."

"Mr. Leland," Captain Ar says, "I think we can help you with your financial issues too. One of my associates here at the post, Bill Shuey, works for Teichmans' Garage downtown. Harry Teichman is looking for a part-time mechanic. Do you have any experience in that line of work?"

I watch Pop's reaction like a buzzard eyeing roadkill. I know he's worked at garages before, but does he have the guts to actually stick to a work schedule this time?

"Well, ma'am," he says, "I'm what you'd call a Jack of all trades and master of none. Yes, I have worked at several garages in my time."

Meemaw reaches over and touches Pop's arm. "Oh, Tom, we sure could use that money."

"You're right," he says to her. "Sure … I'll give it a go," he says to Captain Ar. "When do I start?"

"Just go see Harry when we're finished here," Captain Ar says. "He'll give you the details."

"Wow, Pop," I say, "that's super."

"Yeah, I guess," he mumbles.

"Pockets," Captain Ar says, "you haven't said much today. Do you have any questions or anything at all to say?"

I just shrug. I'm not sure where's she going with the question.

"Have you told your grandmother and dad about the decision you made here last Friday?"

"Oh … no, I haven't."

Meemaw and Pop look at me with a big question mark masking each of their faces.

"Do you think you should?" Captain Ar says. "It's the most important decision anyone must make in his or her life."

"I guess," I say. "I just hadn't thought about telling them."

Meemaw slides to the edge of her seat, and panic drapes her face like a dark cloud. "You're not thinking of moving out to Kansas with your mother, are you?"

Pop stares at me with wide eyes.

"No." I shake my head. "It's nothing like that."

"Well, then, what is it?" Pop says.

I look at Captain Ar. She nods and gives me her reassuring smile.

I turn my attention to Meemaw and Pop. "Last Friday, I asked Jesus to be my Savior. Captain Ar has been telling me about sin and Jesus and that he died on the cross to save us from all our sins. I used to think I just made mistakes, but I never really looked at all the junk in my life as sin. So, I gave my heart and life to God, and I feel much better. And now I know I'll go to heaven some day when I die. And ... I hope you'll do what I did sometime too."

"Oh, that's nice," Meemaw says, relaxing into her chair.

Pop doesn't say anything. He looks like his thoughts are circling the moon again.

Captain Ar says, "Mona and Tom, many years ago, I also accepted Christ as my Savior, and he changed my life drastically. Have either of you ever made that decision?"

"I can't say that I have," Meemaw says.

Pop just shakes his head.

Captain Ar opens up a drawer on her desk and pulls out some small folded papers. "I'd like to give you each something that very clearly explains God's plan of salvation." She hands them each a small folded colorful paper. "I hope you take the time to read that at home. Then you'll better understand what God wants each of us to know and the decision Pockets has made."

"Oh, I'll read it as soon as I go home," Meemaw says.

Pop shoves the paper in back of his pack of cigarettes in his shirt pocket. "Thanks," he says flatly.

"And, Pockets," Captain Ar says, "I have something for you too." She opens the drawer again, pulls out a book, and hands it to me. "It's a devotional for teen girls. As you form the habit of reading the Bible every day, this devotional will help you understand the Bible better."

"Oh, thank you." I look at the book cover and read the title, Daily Devotions for Devoted Teens.

"And one more thing," Captain Ar says to Meemaw and Pop. "It's very important that Pockets go to church. In fact, I believe if you all went as a family, you'd begin to see how that will help your interaction with each other at home."

Meemaw nods with a half-smile. Pop just stares at the woman.

"So, does anyone have any questions about anything?" Captain Ar asks.

"No," Meemaw says while Pop shakes his head.

"I'm good," I say with a big smile.

"Well, before we dismiss, I have something else for Pockets." Captain Ar pushes away and reaches under her desk, pulling up a brand new, red-leather cue stick case. She hands the case to me and says, "This is for you. When I told the kids you were going to compete at the end of the month at the Billiard Emporium, they took up a collection for you to have your own stick. Go on, open the case."

"For me?" I look at Meemaw, who has a big smile lighting up her face, and I glance at Pop, who's back from the moon. "Well," he says, "that was very nice of them."

I zip open the case and pull out two pieces of the most gorgeous dark red and black cue stick I've ever seen. I stand and screw the two pieces together and just about jump out of my skin. "Wow! This is so cool. Thank you!" I babble.

Captain Ar is relaxed in her chair with her arms crossed. "Don't thank me. It was the kids' idea, mainly Leona's and Coochie's."

"That is one beautiful stick," Pop says. "Now make up your mind to shoot smart, and don't let the kids down."

"Oh, I'll do my best," I say. "With this stick, I should be able to clean up."

"And … with God's help," Captain Ar says.

School's been going full force a couple of days already. I've always dreaded school worse than the measles, the dentist, and cleaning my room all rolled up into one. It's never been any fun when other kids avoid you like the plague, and teachers treat you like you have the plague.

But something's different now. I'm sure it has nothing to do with me being in eighth grade, although I do feel a little more grown up since I've got my screwed-up life straightened out with Captain Ar.

For the first time ever, I actually went through my closet and picked out some blouses and skirts that match. I washed and ironed them all too. And Meemaw took me shopping and bought me a brand-new outfit—a black pullover shirt with rhinestones decorating the neckline, a bright blue poodle skirt, and saddle shoes. I felt like a million bucks when I walked into homeroom the first day with my long blonde curls falling perfectly over one eyebrow onto my shoulders. Although most of the kids just gaped at me like I had two heads, a few girls actually said hi to me, and Coochie whistled at me.

Could it be the way I'm looking at things?

I'm sitting in the cafeteria at the seventh and eighth grade lunch period. And although up until this year I always sat alone, Leona, Coochie, and Trudy are sitting with me. Marylou and Pam are actually at the same table—at the other end, of course—engaging in their own giggly world while eyeing the football hunks at the next table. As far as "my hunk," Runner, his lunch break and class schedule are so different from mine, I haven't seen hide nor hair of him at all.

Since it's Friday and the school respects the Catholic students' belief of not eating meat on Fridays, the lunch today is tomato soup and a toasted cheese sandwich with vanilla pudding and chocolate milk, one of my favorite meals. While we all dig in, Leona starts the conversation.

"Pockets, have you been able to practice with your new stick yet? Captain Ar gave us all a sneak peek after she bought it. It's really cool."

"Yeah," I say. "Twice this week after school I went to the post, and me and Captain Ar gave it a good workout. I never knew how much a good stick could improve my game."

Coochie slurps his soup then says, "Improve your game? The way you shoot, I wouldn't think you need any improvement. Maybe that's what I need. I'm lucky to run off three or four balls."

"What's the highest number you've ever run off straight?" Trudy asks. Her Shirley Temple hairdo and cute Kewpie doll features just make me wanna hug her.

"I ran off fifty-four balls straight one time without missing," I say. A few months ago, I would have bragged about that with a burst of cocky pride. Now I feel my face heat up as I feel a flair of humility. I don't want to be the center of attention. I'd rather talk about anything else than me, so I try to change the subject. "Leona, are you ready for the English test on Monday?" Since she's a straight-A student, I already know the answer.

"Yeah, nouns and verbs and the other parts of speech never bother me too much. I should ace it."

"I hate English," Coochie says. "But Dad will tan my hide if I get anything lower than a C. He says I'll never get scholarships to any college no matter how good I can play baseball if I have lousy grades. So I'll be studying all Sunday afternoon."

I wonder what Coochie did to become a member of Captain Ar's army. Trudy, too, for that matter. And it's still a mystery about Leona. She seems so perfect.

"I'm not too bad in English," Trudy says, her cheeks bulging with sandwich. "I get the parts of speech, but when we have to diagram, that's when I bomb out."

"How about you, Pockets?" Leona asks.

I just shake my head while I stir soggy crackers in my soup. "English is the pits for me. I got a D last year for my final grade. I never paid attention in English class, so I'm really hurting. If I don't get passing grades in not only English but in all my subjects, Captain Ar will withdraw me from the pool competition. I just gotta get a grip on this English stuff. Math and History too. I flunked them last year."

"Have you asked Miss Baker to help you at all?" Trudy asks. "I think she's one of the nicest teachers we have. She really cares. My older brother told me that last year she gave him some extra help after school a few days so he could understand conjunctions and interjections better."

"Me and teachers have never gotten along at all," I say. "But I'm starting to see it might have been because of my attitude."

"Miss Baker's really nice," Leona says. "Yesterday I went to her before class started and told her I forgot my homework, and she didn't yell or anything. She just said to have it on her desk the first thing this morning and not to let it happen again."

I finish my soup and work on my sandwich. "I'm going to need all the help I can get. I'm not sure I even know the difference between a noun and a verb."

"Hey, I have an idea," Leona says. "I'll help you. And that will give me a good chance to review too."

"How? When?" I ask.

"It can't be tonight," Trudy says. "It's Friday Fun Night at the post. I wanna see you use your new stick and take Coochie and the boys on a ride to Defeatsville."

"Hardy har har," Coochie says, then digs into his pudding.

"I know!" Leona says to me. "If it's nice tomorrow, how about if I meet you at the park after lunch. I love to study there. It's so quiet. There's nothing but noise at my place with the TV and records blaring and two older brothers arguing all the time. Mom and Dad are on a business trip to Florida, so I'm at the mercy of Charlie and Tim. And the longer I hang around on Saturdays, the more chores they make me do. They think I'm their personal slave."

"Okay," I say. "I'll get all my chores done in the morning. That'll work for me." I wonder what she'd think of my place. I'm not ready to invite anyone to my house yet. Maybe soon. But if Pop would be there recovering from one of his binges, I'd be totally humiliated.

Leona finishes her carton of milk. "Great! Now whatever you do, don't forget your book and all your notes. We're gonna make you an English whiz kid."

"In one study session?" I laugh. "That'll take about twenty years."

"Well, you'll know enough to get through this first test on Monday. We'll worry about the other twenty years later."

"Thanks, you guys," I say to them. "And thanks a lot, Leona."

Leona sifts her fingers through her gorgeous, long, dark curls and pulls them back off her eyebrow. "No problem, my friend. No problem."

Saturday about one o'clock, I coast into the Higher Ups Park picnic pavilion, and I spot Leona already sitting at a table with her English book and notebook. I park my bike, grab my book and notes out of my bike basket, and join Leona.

"Hi," she says. "Are you ready to fry your brain?"

I sit across from her and open my book. "Not really. This is going to be pure torture."

"Aw, it won't be that bad once you get the hang of it. Let's start with the definitions of nouns and verbs."

I'm as anxious to study English as I am to swim the Atlantic Ocean in the middle of an Arctic blast. But I'm more anxious to find out a few things about Leona and my other new friends. "Before we start, can I ask you a question?"

"Sure, what?"

"If you don't want to answer me, it's okay, but … how did you get to be one of Captain Ar's kids?"

Leona stares at her book, and I can tell her thoughts are drifting into her past. Finally she says, "Since we've become friends, I don't mind telling you. In fact, the kids at the post often spill their guts to each other on Friday nights. You'll soon find that out the longer you hang around with us."

I close my book and give her my undivided attention.

"Last Christmas, I tried to kill myself."

I try my best to keep my mouth from dropping open, but I'm sure my face displays complete shock. "What?" Then some of Captain Ar's words stir in my mind, "You never know what's in the heart of anyone who's smiling at you."

"Yep" Leona says. "I overdosed on some of my mother's pain pills. I was in the hospital for a week. That's when Mom and Dad decided it was time to get me some help."

"I-I don't really know what to say. Wow! You always seem like you have it all together."

"Captain Ar has helped me realize how stupid that was. I was just lashing out at my parents to get even with them. I just felt like I was in their way lots of times. With my brothers too. Mom and Dad are always gone on business trips or at meetings. Lots of times, I felt so lonely, I'd cry for hours in my bedroom. My parents have had some counseling, too, and things have gotten better. Once a week they try to include me in something, even if it's just a pizza at Matucci's. I'll never be able to thank Captain Ar. She's become one of my best friends."

"Mine too." I smile then say, "She's helped me so much. She's also told me about Jesus, and I've accepted him as my Savior. I feel so much better about things ... and myself ... and God. Has Captain Ar ever talked to you about Jesus?"

"Yeah, but I haven't really thought too much about what she told me about him."

"You really should. God's always there for you if you want him to be. But it all starts with taking Jesus as your Savior."

"I know," she says and stares at her notes. "I know."

"What about Coochie and Trudy? Do you know why they're in counseling?"

"Yeah. I don't think they'd mind me telling you. All the other kids at the post know."

"I can't imagine what they could have done. They're both too cool."

"Well, Coochie will be the first one to tell you how stupid he was. He and Reuben both were caught shoplifting at Neimonds' clothing store. Last June on a bet by some of their so-called friends, they stashed some neckties under their shirts. A clerk saw them and called the police."

"What about Trudy?"

"Oh, poor Trudy. She didn't get into any trouble. Her mother died last February of cancer, and Trudy couldn't get over it. She started skipping school for days at a time and went into deep, deep depression, locking herself in her bedroom. Her dad got her into counseling with Captain Ar. Trudy says she loves Captain Ar to pieces because she saved her life."

I just nod, having a hard time letting all that I just heard sink in.

"So, Pockets," Leona says, "since we're playing Show and Tell, how did you land in counseling?"

"Other than Captain Ar, I haven't dumped on anyone about my really stupid antics," I say as I ruffle the pages of my book.

"Well, go ahead. And I won't say anything to anyone else. I'll let you do that on Friday nights when you're ready."

I look her straight in the eyes. "I was a member of the Thorns that were busted last June."

Leona is totally shocked, then she breaks out into a hilarious laugh. "You have got to be kidding me. I thought they were all guys in those gangs."

"I guess I was the only girl, but I grew up with all those guys like you did. I just happened to know their dark side and ran with them. You know they all got sent away. Since it was my first offense, the police said counseling was the way to go with me. And am I ever glad. I don't know where I'd be without Captain Ar. She is so cool."

"Wait until I tell Vince this one," she said with a giggle. "He'll never believe it. You! A Thorn!"

I feel my face fire up again, and I ruffle the pages faster. "Oh, please don't tell him. He only knows me from shooting pool at Joe's. He's really a good player."

"Yes, he is. Hey, that reminds me. He's entering that competition at the Billiard Emporium. In fact, when I told him I know you, he asked me if you were going, and I said yes. I told him all about the new cue stick we bought you and everything."

"Oh, really?"

"Yeah, and he said besides you being a pool shark, you are one cute babe."

By now, my cheeks were red hot. "He did?"

"Your face is twenty shades of red!" she says with another round of giggles. "Do you have the hots for him?"

"Oh, mind your own business, and let's get to studying," I babble with a smile.

Leona opens her book and says, "Yeah, I guess we've done enough damage to our egos today. Let's explore the wonderful world of English." She giggles and then says, "Wait until I tell Vince."

CHAPTER THIRTEEN

It's Friday Fun Night, the day before I compete at the Billiard Emporium. Since yesterday my nerves have been playing ping-pong with my muscles, and I hardly slept a wink just thinking about tomorrow. At school, I fought drowsy eyelids all day, but thinking about the competition and waiting to practice with the kids here tonight have given me a super shot of energy.

Captain Ar has just joined me in her office after getting everyone settled in the game room. Although my official counseling sessions are over, I know what she wants.

"So ... Pockets, you probably know what I'd like to ask you." She relaxes into her chair.

"Yes, ma'am." I pull a folded paper out of my pocket and lay it on her desk. "But how do you know every time I have a test?"

"Oh, I have connections. It's hard to keep secrets from me when I care so much about someone." She picks up the paper, starts to unfold it, and says, "I'm very proud of the progress you've made in school. Leona has told me that you two study together quite a bit. And your grandmother said she's seen you studying regularly in your bedroom every evening. That is wonderful."

"Thank you." Earning this woman's approval makes me feel like I've accomplished one of the major milestones of my entire life.

She looks at the paper, then her blue eyes smile at me. "Well, well, well. And you said it was impossible since you had hit rock bottom in history last year. You got a C in this latest test! Good girl. I've been praying you'd pass it. The last thing I wanted to do was call the billiard competition coordinator and withdraw you."

And I know she would have done it in a heartbeat if I had flunked one measly, little test.

"Now …" she says as she hands the test back to me, "I'm hoping you continue with this passing streak all year long and that you aren't just doing it to be able to shoot in the competition." She stares and waits for my answer.

"I promise I'll do my best. I'm really starting to like school for the first time ever. I'm finding that the teachers aren't all members of the 'Out to Get the Leland Kid Club.' Miss Baker, my English teacher, even said she's never seen any student make such a turnaround as me, and she said it in front of the whole class after I got a B on that punctuation test last week."

"One thing I want you to remember is that God has given you a good mind, Pockets. And I'm so thankful you're starting to use it the way God intended. He's also given you the skill to shoot pool well. Don't forget that either."

"Okay, I won't."

"Before we join the kids, I want to ask you how things are going at home."

"At home?"

"Yes. Is your dad working at the garage?"

"Yep, and so far, so good," I say with a sigh. "I think he's only showed up late once because he was shooting pool into the wee hours the night before."

"Did he find a shooting partner?"

I can't help but chuckle. "Yeah. Believe it or not, he paired up with griping Jake. And they've been on a roll."

"Griping Jake?"

"Oh, that's Jake Dombroski. He works at the foundry. He always makes excuses when he loses games, although lately he's probably been parking his complaints since him and Pop are cleaning everybody up."

Captain Ar leans forward on her desk. "And how's your grandmother doing? You said you worry about her because she works so hard, and she's always so tired."

"Oh, she's okay, I guess. But the other day when she was carrying a heavy bucket of coal into the house, I saw her grabbing her chest like she had a sharp pain or something. I ran to her side and took the coal bucket and told her to sit down. But she said she was okay and just lost her breath for a minute."

"You keep an eye on her and help her as much as you can."

"I do … I will."

"Have you heard from your mother?"

"No, but I guess she's settled in with Aunt Alma. I sent her a letter and told her all about me getting saved, and I even sent her the little paper you gave Meemaw. I told Mom about the billiard competition too."

"Have you been able to tell your folks that you love them? And I mean with words not just your actions."

"I'm working on that," I say as I squirm in my seat. I'm getting antsy as I think of all the time I'm missing not shooting pool right now. Then, I remember something really important to tell the woman. "Oh, I've been wanting to tell you that me and Meemaw went to church last Sunday. Pop couldn't get up and go with us because he was out so late the night before."

"I'm very glad to hear that you went. Did you like it?"

"Yeah. I went to the teen class for Sunday school, and most of the kids were really friendly. In fact, Reuben was there, and he introduced me to everybody. Later in the church service, the preacher said just about all the same stuff you've been telling me. It was cool."

Captain Ar nods with a big smile. "That's great, Pockets. The older you get, the more you'll be glad you went to church and learned about God."

"The preacher also said how important it is to read the Bible every day, just like you told me. I'm trying real hard to do that … and I like the devotional book you gave me too."

"Good. Did your grandmother say anything about the services?"

"Nah. She keeps saying she wants to get me to church because that's what you said we should do. I'm not sure it's that important to her."

"Well, you just be a big help to her and your dad, so they see the difference in your life since you accepted Jesus. They'll realize it's God who changed you, and they'll want that change in their lives too." She pushes away from the desk and stands. "Now, let's go get you ready for tomorrow. Oh, I almost forgot." She reaches into a desk drawer and pulls out a brochure. "This schedule just arrived in the mail yesterday. It has the categories defined with all the competitors listed. It looks like there are only two teen girls entered, so they've lumped you in the teen category with eight boys. I didn't think that would be an issue with you since you've been shooting against males of all ages for years—and beating them."

I just nod and smile at her.

"And I noticed there's a fellow from our area in the teen category. His name is Vince Ramsey. Do you know him?"

Do I know him? Do I ever! "Yes, ma'am. He shoots at Joe's all the time."

"Well, you just might face him tomorrow if you both keep winning and advance to the final bracket. Wouldn't that be a hoot?"

Woman, you have no idea. "Yes, ma'am. Do you know he's Leona's cousin?"

"Really? Well, then I imagine Leona and her family will be going to support him."

"Wow, if Leona's there, how's she gonna root for both of us at the same time?"

Captain Ar laughs. "That I've got to see."

"Do you think it's all right if I wear my Phillies T-shirt and jeans tomorrow?"

She shuffles through the brochure. "I didn't see anything about a dress code, so I think you'll be fine. You're not going to wear your hat, are you?"

"Nah," I say. "I'm beyond that. I'll just wear my hair in a ponytail when I'm shooting."

"That'll work. And remember to tell your folks we'll leave here at six-thirty tomorrow morning. We want to be at the Billiard Emporium no later than nine o'clock to get you signed in. And I'm sure you don't want to miss Ruth McGinnis's exhibition at nine-thirty."

"No, ma'am. I can't wait to see her." As I head toward the game room, Captain Ar wraps her arm around my shoulders.

"You just do your best tomorrow, and God will be pleased whether you win or lose. You're a good kid, Pockets, and I'm very proud of you."

And with my very best friend in the whole, wide world at my side, I feel like I could run all the way to Philadelphia.

At ten after nine the next morning, we pulled into the Billiard Emporium in downtown Philly. Meemaw had packed some snacks and water for us, so we only lost a few minutes for a quick pit stop along the way.

After Captain Ar prayed in the car for God to help me do my best, we went into the huge, fancy building that looked as big as a football field. After we checked out the restrooms, me and Captain Ar reported to the registration desk. From there, we were directed to go to the main floor where thirteen pool tables are stationed and encircled by rows of bleachers along the walls.

All I can say is "Wow!"

Each table with its spotless velvety-green cloth already has its fifteen shiny balls set to break. A few feet above each table hang two really cool Tiffany lights suspended on long golden chains. In the center of the large room stands the thirteenth table. The room is fast filling with a flow of gabbing pool lovers climbing on the bleachers closest to the center table where we were told Ruth McGinnis would have her exhibition.

"Hey, you guys!"

I pivot and look behind me. Leona is standing there with two older people and Runner! My face flushes red hot like I've been running a mile, and I just stare at him.

"Well, hello, Leona," Captain Ar says.

"Hi, everybody!" She raises her hand toward those with her. "This is my cousin Vince and my aunt and uncle."

The man who looks like an older version of Runner with graying hair and a pencil-thin mustache extends his hand toward Pop. "I'm Clayton Ramsey. This is my wife, Pauline."

"How do you do," Pop says and shakes the man's hand.

"Hello." Mrs. Ramsey nods. Although inches shorter than her guys, she's a looker with a blonde page boy hairdo, makeup applied to perfection, and a navy blue jacket and matching straight skirt.

Captain Ar introduces herself, Pop, Meemaw, and me. While the grown-ups make small talk, Runner directs his attention toward me.

"How are you, Pockets? Are you nervous?"

"I would be a nervous wreck," Leona says as she and Runner move closer to me.

I feel my face heat up big time. "I-I'm a little nervous," I say as I stare into his dreamy chocolate brown eyes. "How about you?"

"Yeah, but Dad says a little nerves are good. It'll help me concentrate more if I don't think I'm a big shot and can just walk in here and take over."

He smiles at me, and goose bumps ripple up and down my spine. I just stare and smile back.

"I see we're in the same teen category," Runner says. "Wouldn't it be a riot if we face each other in the finals? Just like old times at Joe's."

"Yeah, that would be something," I say.

"Attention, everyone!" A loud speaker blares. "Ruth McGinnis will start her exhibition in ten minutes. Please find your seats."

We all head toward an empty section of bleachers and settle in. Runner stations himself on one side of me, and Leona sits on my other side, and I'm about to watch my pool idol, the Queen of Billiards, show her stuff. If there's such a thing as Pool Heaven, I'm in it.

In a few minutes, a woman carrying a black cue case comes out of a side door and approaches the center table. The crowd stands to its feet and applauds to the high hilt for Ruth McGinnis. She's a little taller than I imagined, her dark hair in a plain-Jane short wavy style. Her slim figure is touting a frilly white blouse and a gray jacket with a matching pleated skirt. Her shoes are the same as Captain Ar wears. High heels wouldn't cut it here. You gotta be comfortable shooting pool.

As the loud speaker introduces the pool shark and fires off a few of her many achievements in the billiard world, including shooting over a hundred straight without missing, Ruth unzips her cue case, screws her stick together, and warms up by running off an entire rack of balls. Then for the next forty-five minutes she wows the crowd, including me with my mouth stuck in the open mode. With out-of-sight cue ball control, she shows us trick shots that look impossible to make, including jumping the cue ball over three other balls to make a fourth ball in a corner pocket.

As I watch every amazing shot, I wonder why I've never seen anything about her in my billiard magazines. She's every bit as good as any of the men pros like Willie Mosconi. I guess us gals have to band together and make our mark in this "men only" billiard world.

Ruth's exhibition ends, the crowd gives her a "standing O," and a stream of fans rush toward her for her autograph.

"Would you like to meet her?" Captain Ar says to me as we make our way off the bleachers.

"Would I ever!" I say.

Pop has a different idea. "I noticed they have a cafeteria somewhere over on that side of the building." He points toward the one exit and checks his watch. "Anybody in the mood for something to eat? It's a little after eleven and almost lunchtime."

"Yes," Mr. Ramsey says. "We didn't have much this morning. Let's do it."

"I could eat a hamburger or pizza," Runner says.

"Me too," Leona says. "Let's hurry before the line gets too long."

"You all go ahead," Captain Ar says. "I'm going with Pockets to meet Ruth and get her autograph. We'll meet up with you in the cafeteria later."

"Okay," Meemaw says. "Pockets, do you have money for lunch?"

"I—"

"That's all right, Mona," Captain Ar says. "I've got her covered."

"Thank you so much," Meemaw says to her.

"Yeah, thanks!" I say.

After waiting in line forty-five minutes, I get to meet Ruth. She grabs a flyer with her picture on it from a pile on a small table and signs the picture "To Pockets, Go for it, the Billiard Queen." I am thrilled beyond words when she actually takes the time to talk to me.

"So, young lady, are you a fan of pool?"

"Y-Yes, ma'am, I like to shoot."

Captain Ar and Ruth shake hands. "Ruth, I'm Captain Arlene Masters from the Salvation Army Post in Ashland. I called you a week ago and told you about Pockets." Captain Ar gives me a quick shoulder hug. "She's quite the pool player already at fourteen."

Ruth stares into space for a few seconds then says, "Oh, yes! I do remember your phone call." She extends her hand to me, and we shake.

Wow, I'm touching a girl billiard genius! "It's so nice to meet you."

Captain Ar adds, "As I had told you, Pockets is competing in the teen category this afternoon. Besides her, there's only one other girl going up against eight teenage boys."

Ruth gives me a smile that almost equals Captain Ar's best one. "Well, Pockets, how would you like another fan there to root you on? I've been asked to present the trophies to the winners at the end of the competition, so I'll be watching as many matches as I can."

"You'd like to watch m-me?" I mumble.

"We gals have to stick together, don't we?" she says.

I just nod and stare.

"We sure do," Captain Ar says.

"Go get 'em, tiger," Ruth says to me.

"Thank you," I say again as me and Captain Ar turn away and head to the cafeteria.

And I thought my nerves were ready to ship out before.

CHAPTER FOURTEEN

It's four o'clock. Since one o'clock, twelve pool tables have buzzed with different age groups battling it out in double-elimination eight ball. Three of the tables in the far end of the humongous room hosted the ten teens, two on each table at a time.

Me and the other girl, Helen, didn't face each other until about two o'clock. Earlier, we had both moved to the losers' brackets. I had lost to some guy named Bubba, the perfect name for the much older teen, built like an army tank with arms as big as my thighs. And, brother, can he shoot.

I got myself under control and won the match against Helen, two games outright, and moved on to the final bracket for the champion match.

And, yes, Runner made it there too. He had sent Bubba on his merry way.

As we chalk up for our three-game match at the center table, Runner comes to me and whispers, "May the best man win," and we both laugh.

I take a deep breath and gaze at the excited crowd packed on the bleachers. I spot Meemaw, Pop, and Captain Ar, sitting with the Ramseys and Leona. Leona sees me looking her way, raises her hands, and gives me a look as if to say, "I'm sunk no matter who I cheer for." Next to her sits Ruth.

My nerves have just about had it and are about ready to crash, but I lecture them about getting their act together. I look at the rows and rows of onlookers, their eyes focused on every move I make. I'm hoping they're rooting for me and every other girl who would love to shoot pool when times change, and when us gals are welcomed to the game.

The loud speaker introduces Runner and me as we chalk up and shoot a few practice balls. When the announcer says my name, some nut from the bleachers yells out over the applause, "Hey girlie, girl, why don't you go home to your apron and kitchen where you belong!"

My face flushes red hot as I ignore the ignorant remark then feel much better when two men in blue uniforms escort the big mouth out, and the crowd cheers them on.

Our match begins, and Runner gets to break the first game, winning the coin tossed by the referee. Runner goes on to run his seven solid-colored balls but misses the eight ball, a very tough bank shot. He hands the game to me on a silver platter.

Score: Leland—one; Ramsey—zero.

As fate would have it, I break the second game, but I don't make one stinkin' ball. This time Runner cleans up, shooting all of his seven balls and the eight ball.

Score: Leland—one; Ramsey—one.

By now the crowd is going wild, cheering us both on. I glance at the bleachers and spot a sign someone is holding up that reads GIRL POWER. I smile then shift my attention to Meemaw and the others sitting with her. Leona still has a flabbergasted look on her face, but Captain Ar is smiling and gives me a thumbs-up.

It's Runner's turn to break the third game, which decides the match, the trophy, and the hundred dollars. He smacks the cue ball into the rack and makes one striped ball and one solid ball.

I study the layout of the table, and the balls aren't spread very well. Some are still clustered together like a nest of eggs, and he's got some really tough combinations to make if he's gonna clear the table. I can tell by the look on his face he's worried.

Sure enough, he misses his next shot when he tries one of the tough combinations. But what he did was open the table up for me to run all solid balls and the eight ball with no trouble.

As I study the table and my next few shots, I hear a chant start up in the crowd: "Go, Pockets, go! Go, Pockets, go!" I have no doubt Leona and Captain Ar got everybody going on that one.

I chalk up and steady my nerves. I start to shoot and run off all my balls with only the eight ball left resting inches from a corner pocket. The shot's so easy I can make it blindfolded.

As I concentrate on the table, I take a quick glance at Runner, who's giving me his best smile. Then … he winks at me with those chocolate brown eyes, and I lose it. My heart takes off toward Runner, and when I shoot, I miscue, sending the cue ball into the side pocket. Game over, and it's in Runner's lap.

An echo of moans and groans from the crowd settles over me like a wet blanket. I can't believe it. I lost the game and the match. I hope Meemaw and Pop can be happy with the second-place fifty dollars.

As the loud speaker announces Runner's victory and the awards ceremony to take place in a few minutes, Runner rushes to my side. "Pockets, I'm so sorry."

I feel like he really means it. "If I had to lose, I'm glad it was to you," I say tearing up. The last thing I want is to be branded a bawl baby and a sore loser. "Good job," I add then I casually wipe my eyes as we unscrew our sticks and pack them in their cases.

In a few minutes, the Billiard Queen joins Runner and me as we stand before the crowd. Speaking into a floor microphone, Ruth presents Runner with his trophy amidst a round of applause. Next, she hands me a foot-tall shiny trophy with an eight ball emblem on the top, and the crowd applauds again. Runner even joins in as our smiles connect.

Ruth then makes a mini-speech that will lodge itself forever in my brain cells, "And second place goes to Tommi Jo Leland, better known as Pockets in her billiard world. Ladies and gentlemen, with talented young ladies like Pockets, it's my hope that we gals will soon be welcome in poolrooms across the land. Billiards is fast losing its stigma of being a dirty game played only in dark places frequented by gamblers and those of ill repute. For all you gals out there who would love to learn to shoot, you go for it. Improve your game, learn to shoot as well as Pockets, and together we females can change the game and the places it's played."

Although we arrived home on Saturday early enough to get a good night's sleep, me and Meemaw don't make church on Sunday. She said she didn't feel well and wanted to rest all day. And Pop disappeared after we got home on Saturday, so I figured I wouldn't see him for a day or so. I was right.

The rest of the week racked up the strangest events I've ever had in my life. I went from flying high as a kite in a crisp, autumn wind to sinking as low as a hundred-pound rock in a pond.

First thing Monday morning in homeroom, big mouth Leona announces to the whole class that I came in second at the billiard competition and won fifty dollars and a trophy.

A few of the boys can't believe that a girl would even know how to hold a cue stick, so they brush off the whole thing as a bunch of baloney.

Our homeroom teacher, Miss Weber, is so skeptically impressed with me that she makes me promise to bring in my trophy, which I do the very next day. I really think deep down in my heart that because of my reputation of telling a string of whoppers in seventh grade, she didn't really believe the story either and wanted to put me on the spot. Boy, was she ever surprised!

And so was everybody else.

My fame spreads through the junior high like wildfire, and for the first time in my pathetic life, I am "somebody." In every class and at lunch period, student after student, even the football players, cheerleaders, and some teachers, congratulate me and wow over the trophy that I pull out of my bookbag everywhere I go.

Despite Captain Ar's reminding me last Friday to give God the credit, I get a big head and drink in all the attention like the best root beer float I could ever taste. By Thursday, Leona gets sick of me and the pride that oozes out all over me like poison ivy pus. To tell you the truth, I even get sick of me.

When I get home and hide out in my bedroom, I pull out the trophy, set it on my dresser, say "big deal," and ask God to forgive me. For some reason, all the glitter and gold and attention I had received all week loses its flair. And although I'm still happy as all get out that I came in second, it's not as important to me as it had been.

Captain Ar had said that "things of the earth" only satisfy for a while, but Jesus fills the hole in a person's heart all the time. I'm starting to understand a little what she means. And the trophy suddenly takes a back seat in my life for another reason—a letter from Mom that I see lying on my bed. I stretch out on the bed, rip the envelope open, and read.

Dear Tommi Jo,

I'm so sorry it's taken me so long to write to you. I'm settled in with your Aunt Alma and have a job at the candy factory.

Since I share expenses with your aunt, I've already started getting caught up on some bills that I still have in PA. I like my job. I'm on an assembly line rolling coconut balls in a pool of dark chocolate. It's kinda fun, but the worst part is standing for eight hours every day.

I looked at the church paper you sent me, and I'm glad you've got some religion in your life. I'm sure God can help you get your grades up in school. I hope you showed that paper to your father before you sent it to me. He really needs that a lot more than I do.

Let me know how you do in the pool competition.

Your aunt has a pretty nice place here in Kansas. She's worked very hard since your Uncle Frank died, and it's paid off. Her ranch-style house in the suburbs has three bedrooms. We had a real good talk the other day, and she said she wouldn't mind if I asked you to move here with us. There's a nice school just six blocks from her house. I know the idea of you moving here will go over with your grandmother like a lead balloon. And as far as what your dad thinks, I really don't care.

I want you to think about whether you'd like to try living with us and go to a new school and make some friends. Maybe a fresh start is what you need in your life too. Your aunt and I are planning to drive home for Thanksgiving. You could come home with me then. Write and let me know what you think about all of this.

Love,

Mother

That does it. I miss my mom. I've always missed her since she and dad split. I bury my head in my arms and bawl like there's no tomorrow. Can there really be a "tomorrow" with my mother?

It's Friday Fun Night, and I bring the trophy to show the kids.

After they fall all over me with their compliments and pats on the back and we have snack time, I ask to see Captain Ar alone while the kids settle in to their games.

Sitting in front of Captain Ar at her desk, I hand her Mom's letter. While she reads, I stare at the woman who has been like the mother I never had. I love her more than I thought I could love anyone and want to be like her. How can I leave the person who straightened out my stupid, messy life and introduced me to Jesus? Yeah, I cry again, and tears dribble down my face just thinking of leaving Ashland, Meemaw, Pop, my new friends, Runner … and Captain Ar.

She looks at me, and her blue eyes get moist. "Well, Pockets. This is quite the letter."

I nod and wipe my eyes.

"Did you show this to your grandmother and dad?"

"Not yet. I know they'll hit the ceiling and say there's no way I'm moving to Kansas."

"Honey, what do you want to do?"

I just shrug.

"I think I know how you feel. Remember I told you I grew up in a home very much like yours? I believe in the heart of every kid is the desire to love their mother and feel that love returned. I know that's been missing in your life."

I sniffle and stare deep into her soul. I can almost feel the hurt she grew up with and finally realize why she understands me so well.

She hands me a wad of tissues. "This is a very big decision you need to make. I suggest you pray about this every day for a while. You have some time to decide before Thanksgiving gets here. And you need to tell your folks soon."

"I know it's a big decision. And it's really hard because I'm just beginning to like school. For the first time in my life, I have friends. Meemaw and Pop need me. And ... I-I don't want to leave ... you."

Captain Ar leans forward with sparkling blue eyes and points at me. "I would miss you very much if you move. But, Pockets, you are such a young Christian, I know you're still learning to follow the Lord's leading in your life. This is a time when you want to do what you believe God wants you to do. And you'll only get that peace in your heart as you read his Word and pray for direction. He will give it to you. I promise. Let's pray about this right now."

We exchange smiles, and she closes with a prayer that makes me feel like the answer is already on the way.

CHAPTER FIFTEEN

"Tommi Jo Leland, please report to the principal's office."

On the second Wednesday in October, it's quarter after two, and I'm sitting in English class when I hear that announcement blast over the intercom. Miss Baker nods at me, and I grab all my books, hightail it out of the room, and practically run to the principal's office.

I break out in a cold sweat, wondering what I could have done to get me in such big trouble. As far as I know, I've kept my nose clean and have passed every test since school started. I've been listening to every word Captain Ar says and trying to read my Bible and devotional every day. I only hang out with the "good gang" at the post every Friday night. Me and Meemaw have even been going to church, and I'm making new friends there.

Maybe the cops want to haul me off for having such a big head last month over my pool victory.

I rush into the principal's waiting room. The secretary behind the counter forces out a smile and gestures to her right, to the row of chairs along the wall.

Captain Ar is seated there. She hurries to me, worry draped all over her face. "Pockets, your grandmother is in intensive care at the Ashland General Hospital. Your dad just called me to come get you. He said she was doing the breakfast dishes this morning and just collapsed. He called the emergency number, and the ambulance came in a few minutes and transported her to the hospital. She had a heart attack."

I stand glued to the floor and try to let what I've just heard sink in to my panicking brain. "Meemaw? A heart attack?"

"Yes," she says. "I've already signed you out. Go get your jacket and anything else you need from your locker and meet me out front. We'll go to see her right away."

In twenty minutes, we're sitting in the waiting room outside the ICU, and Pop's at the nurses' station asking for permission to let me see Meemaw. He pokes back his glasses and comes to us, accompanied by a thin, gray-haired man in a white coat with a stethoscope around his neck.

"I'm Doctor Kraft," the man says and shakes Captain Ar's hand.

"I'm Arlene Masters from the Ashland Salvation Army post," she says. "I'm a friend of the family."

"This is my daughter, Tommi Jo," Pop tells the doctor. "We live with Mona."

"I see," the doctor says. "We usually don't allow children in the ICU. However, since this young lady is fourteen and is such a close relative, she may go in."

"Thank you." Pop pokes back his glasses again. He always does that when he's a nervous wreck. He looks at the doctor and then at me with a mask of fear like I've never seen on him before.

"Is she gonna be all right?" I ask.

"It's hard to tell," the doctor says. "Right now it's touch and go. We've done all we can to make her comfortable. For a gal in her sixties, she's in good shape, and all the tests show the treatment for her aortic aneurysm will depend on its cause, its size and location, and the factors that put her at risk. Small aneurysms like hers may be managed with healthy lifestyle changes or medicine. The goal is to slow the growth of the aneurysm and lower the chance of rupture or dissection."

"Oh, that's super news, isn't it, Pop?" I say.

"Yes. Is it all good news?" Pop asks the doctor.

"Well, we've run tests to check her for high blood pressure, coronary heart disease, kidney disease, and high blood cholesterol. If they come back negative, she has a good chance of bouncing back with just prescribed medications. She's fortunate that smoking isn't an issue either. I understand she does work full-time. As long as her job doesn't require heavy lifting, she might even be able to work, although maybe just part-time."

"Can I see her?" I ask.

"Yes," the doctor says. "Two at a time may go in."

"You two go ahead," Pop says to me and Captain Ar. "I've been with her since they got her settled in here."

"Now don't be alarmed at what you see," the doctor says. "She's hooked up to all kinds of machines, and she has an oxygen mask on. A word of caution here. Please do not try to talk to her. She's heavily medicated and needs her rest. She probably wouldn't hear you anyway. As long as you stay quiet, you can sit by her side for as long as you want."

"Thank you, Doctor," Captain Ar says.

Doctor Kraft turns to walk away. "If you have any questions, just relay them to the nurses' station, and we'll get back to you as soon as possible."

"Thanks again," Pop says to the doctor then turns to me. "Pockets, I'm going home for a while. When your grandma collapsed, she tried to catch herself and pulled the dish drainer down with some dishes in it. They smashed all over the floor. It's lucky she didn't get cut real bad. I want to clean up that mess and grab a bite to eat. I need to call your mother and tell her what happened. Then I'll try to come back for you in about an hour-and-a-half."

"Okay, Pop."

"Tom," Captain Ar says, "After Pockets and I visit Mona, how about if I bring Pockets home. She'll need a break and something to eat too, and I must get back to the office. You two can come back in the evening."

"That's a good idea. I appreciate your help, Arlene. I'll see you in a little while, Pockets." Pop pokes back his glasses and walks away.

"I'll see you later, Pop."

Captain Ar gives me a shoulder hug. "Let's go see your grandma."

We carefully open the door and walk into the ICU like we're walking on eggs. Doctor Kraft wasn't kidding when he said Meemaw was wired to machines. She's lying perfectly still and reminds me of a movie I saw where a robot was being plugged into machines to give him the power to move.

Me and Captain Ar cautiously approach the bed. I spot a chair next to the bed and another chair along the one wall.

"Go ahead and sit in that chair next to her," Captain Ar whispers and heads to the chair along the wall.

I sit and stare at Meemaw and watch her shallow breathing. Her face is so pale, it scares me. I think if she could see what she looks like, she'd demand to have her makeup case. I reach and gently touch her hand, and it's cold. My eyes flood with tears as I think about what life would be like without my Meemaw, who cared for me so much when Mom walked out on me.

When I sniffle and wipe my tears on my arm, Captain Ar gives me some tissues, then stands behind me with her hands on my shoulders. "Pockets," she says. "This is the time when your faith in God is put to the test. You have to just pray for his perfect will for your grandma."

As always, I listen to what the woman is saying with every cell in my body. Then I open up my heart to God and beg him to save my Meemaw's life … if it is his will.

In an hour-and-a-half, Captain Ar whispers, "Pockets, I think we should probably get you home. I'll give you a few minutes yet while I wait outside."

"All right," I say, never taking my gaze off Meemaw.

Captain Ar leaves but returns in a few seconds. "Pockets, some kids are outside waiting to see you."

"Some kids?"

"Yes."

"Okay," I say to her then whisper to Meemaw, "I'll see you later, Meemaw. I love you."

I leave the room and am greeted by "some kids" while Captain Ar stands by. The kids are friends. My friends. A few months ago, I couldn't have said that. I look at each one and can't believe they're here. I'm beginning to learn what friendship really means.

Leona's smiling and carrying a vase of pink and red rose buds. With her are Coochie, Reuben, Trudy … and Runner! All are forcing out smiles mixed with looks of concern.

Leona hugs me and hands me the flowers. "These are for your gram."

"Thanks, guys," I say. "But how did you know?"

"Pockets," Captain Ar says, "let me have the flowers, and I'll put them in the room."

I hand her the vase, and she goes in and out of Meemaw's room in a few seconds.

"We heard about your gram through the grapevine at school," Coochie says.

"So we wanted to come and support you," Reuben says, and Trudy nods.

I look at Runner, whose gaze locks on mine. "We're all very sorry about your grandma. What can we do to help?"

"You're helping me right now by being here," I say. "I really appreciate it."

Reuben raises his index finger and says, "My mom said if we call our pastor about this, the ladies of the church will send in some meals for you and your dad."

"That's a wonderful idea," Captain Ar says.

Reuben adds, "And Mom said Pastor Sutcliff plans to visit your gram if you and your dad think it's a good idea."

"I'd really like the pastor to do that," I say.

Captain Ar steps next to my side. "Well, kids, I promised Pockets' dad that I'd have her home about now, so we better get going. Thank you all for your love and concern for Pockets and her family."

"What are friends for?" Leona says, and the rest nod.

"C'mon," Captain Ar says. "We can all walk to the parking lot together."

Runner steps next to me and says, "And let us all know how your gram is doing."

"I sure will," I say. "And you'll be the first one I tell."

On the way home, me and the woman don't say much at all. I'm worried to death and keep praying for God to make Meemaw better. A few miles from home Captain Ar finally shares her thoughts.

"Honey, are you all right?"

"I guess, but I'm so worried about Meemaw."

"Do you believe God is in control of this situation?"

"Kinda."

"Listen to this verse that has given me comfort when trouble has come my way. The verse is found in Romans, chapter eight, verse twenty-eight. 'And we know that all things work together for good to them that love God, to them who are the called according to his purpose.' Do you understand what that means?"

"I think so. If we trust in God through even the bad times, he'll work it out somehow for the good. But how can Meemaw having a heart attack be anything good?"

"That remains to be seen. We don't know what the future holds. We just have to trust that God will work this out for his glory and our good."

"I want to believe that."

"If God raises up your grandmother, she's going to need a lot of help. She might not be able to go back to work for a while, or maybe not at all. I have a friend who had the same kind of heart issues, and she wasn't allowed do anything strenuous for a month."

"I just have to be there for her. And I hope Pop will forget about disappearing for days at a time. We'll need him at home more than ever."

"Had you given any more thought over the last few weeks about moving in with your mother?"

"Yeah, I thought about it and prayed an awful lot about it, but this thing with Meemaw just changed everything. If Meemaw makes it and comes home, I'm going to write Mom or even call her and tell her I need to stay here. Maybe by next summer if Meemaw is all better, I could go visit Mom and Aunt Alma for a few weeks."

"Now that's an idea. That would give you a good taste of how it would be to live with them."

"I keep thinking how I'd feel to be a few weeks away from Meemaw and Pop ... and my friends ... and you. That's about all I probably could handle before going bonkers."

"And how about church? From what you've told me, neither your mom or aunt are church goers."

"No, but I keep praying they will soon start."

Captain Ar pulls the car in front of my house, idles the car, and looks at me. "Pockets, before you leave, let me ask you a question. Why do you want to go to church?"

"Huh?"

"How have you changed? You had no time for God nor church a few months ago."

I sit and think deep ... really deep. "I guess because I asked Jesus into my life, and he gave me the desire to go to church and read the Bible."

"All right. Here's another question. Why does your grandmother go to church?"

"She says it's so I can get there because you said it would be good for me."

"So, as far as you know, she's never accepted Christ as her Savior?"

I slowly shake my head. "I don't think so. She never says anything about God, and I don't see her reading the Bible or anything like that."

"Have you ever talked to her about it? And how about your dad?"

I shake my head no again. "I've wanted to, but with the billiard competition and school starting and everything, I was too busy."

"Maybe everything has slowed down in your life now so you can talk to her and your dad about Jesus."

With my mind racing full speed ahead I nod. "If Meemaw does recover, it'll be the first thing I want to talk to her about."

"That's great. And when Pastor Sutcliff visits her, I'm sure that's one thing he'll want to discuss with her and your dad too. There's nothing more important in life than knowing if you're going to heaven, is there?"

"No," I say. "Nothing more important."

Thursday and Friday, I go to school while Pop works at the garage. And he's not been missing any days nor even reporting late. I make him promise to call the hospital every few hours to see how Meemaw's doing and to come get me if we need to be by her side. I have a really hard time concentrating on anything but the clock, waiting for school to be out so I can go see her. Captain Ar also makes periodic visits to Meemaw and promises to let me know anything that's important.

When we go to the hospital, Doctor Kraft gives us an upbeat report each time. Friday has the best news ever.

"She's recovering nicely, and she's off the oxygen and IV. She might even feel well enough to sit up soon and have some real food. She's going to make it, but we'll be monitoring her blood pressure and lipids and addressing any other medical issues. Of course, her diet and exercise will be modified. Usually people in her condition go back to work in four to six weeks and just limit their stress and heavy lifting. We'll follow up with tests in six months and then a year to make sure the aneurysm doesn't change or increase. Tomorrow if she keeps recovering at her present rate, we'll move her to the Skilled Care Unit."

Yep, that's the best news ever.

When me and Pop get home Friday afternoon, I call my friends, Runner first. Then, I heat up some amazing macaroni and cheese that one of the church ladies had given us for supper. When I ask Pop when we're leaving for the hospital, he has a different idea.

"Pockets, I think you need a break. Why don't you go to the post tonight and have some fun with your friends. It'll be good for you to shoot some pool and park your worries for a while. I'll go sit with your grandma after I drop you off at the post. I'll come back for you at nine o'clock."

To tell you the truth, shooting pool had been the furthest thing from my worried mind. But I figured to be with my friends and Captain Ar definitely would help my mental state. So I agree, and at seven o'clock I walk into the back room of the post.

Captain Ar with her super smelling perfume greets me with a hug as all the kids and Bill huddle around the counter in the kitchenette with big smiles plastered all over their faces. And ... Runner is here too!

Has he joined the woman's troop?

Captain Ar leads me to the counter loaded with snacks and a big, fancy cake decorated with the words, We're praying for your gram.

"What's all this?" I'm stupefied.

"We just wanted to encourage you," Captain Ar says.

"Captain Ar invited me here tonight," Runner says. "I told her I wouldn't miss it for even a solid gold cue ball."

Everyone laughs.

"Yeah." Leona hands me a sealed envelope. "We thought you needed some cheering up. Here's a card for you. Open it."

"Now?"

"Now," Coochie says.

I look at the row of smiling faces, then open the envelope and look at a really neat card with a picture on the front of an autumn scene of golden trees, a waterfall, and a pink sunset. I open the card, and I grab a bunch of money before the bills fall all over the place.

"The kids wanted to give you something to help with expenses," Captain Ar says. "We know your dad could probably use some gas money. I said they could do it on one condition. They couldn't ask their parents for the money. They had to use their own allowances or earn the cash themselves."

"I cut some lawns," Reuben says.

"I babysat," Trudy says.

"There's thirty-two dollars and seventy-six cents there," Captain Ar says.

"I robbed my piggy bank for the seventy-six cents," Coochie says, and everyone laughs again.

"Wow! Thanks, guys," I say. "It will help a lot."

"Bill, will you offer a prayer, and we'll dig in," Captain Ar says.

After Bill prays, we have our snacks, play games until nine o'clock, and the love for me in the room wraps around me like a warm blanket.

Saturday morning, me and Pop grab a quick cereal breakfast at home then head to the hospital. I take all my school books to do my homework when Meemaw can't help but doze off and on during the day.

She's now in the Skilled Care Unit.

When we get there, Meemaw's sitting up in bed but snoring like a bear in hibernation, so we sneak in, and I situate myself next to her and work on my books. Pop settles into a chair along the wall, and for the next hour or so, Meemaw sleeps, Pop reads magazines, and I do some of my homework and read my Bible and devotional.

The door slowly opens and Doctor Kraft gestures for me and Pop to join him outside. When we do, the doctor is smiling.

"I have good news for you," he says. "Everything we had hoped would happen did happen. Her aneurysm is small and behaving itself. All her vitals are good, and she's eating well. We plan to discharge her tomorrow morning."

I'm so excited I have to hold back from shouting and hugging the man.

"That's wonderful," Pop says. "What time should we be here?"

"She should be ready to go at ten o'clock. Now remember, for a month she's to do nothing but rest. If she wants to do anything around the house, that will be okay but only small tasks like washing the dishes, and then only as long as there's no heavy lifting anything at all."

"We'll be watching her carefully," Pop says.

"And some of the ladies from church are going to come to the house and help with cleaning and cooking," I say.

"Good," Doctor Kraft says. "I'll want to see her once a week for a while, but the way it looks right now, she can probably go back to work maybe in six weeks or so."

"Thank you, doctor," Pop says.

"Sure. I'll be checking on her in my afternoon rounds. Goodbye now." He turns and heads down the hallway.

"Goodbye," we both say, smile at each other, and head back into the room.

Meemaw is wide awake. "Well," she says, "I've been wondering where you two have been hiding."

"Oh, Meemaw!" I rush to her side and give her a big, fat hug. "I'm so glad you're going to be okay."

"Gave you two a pretty good scare, did I?" She smiles.

"You're not kidding," Pop says. "But we just talked to Doctor Kraft. You're going home tomorrow."

Meemaw rubs her cheeks and says, "Well, don't forget my makeup case. I looked in the mirror in the bathroom and was half scared out of my wits."

"We'll remember to bring it," I say. "But you look beautiful just the way you are."

For the next few hours we chat, and at noon, the nurse brings in Meemaw's lunch. Me and Pop decide to go to the hospital's cafeteria for a quick bite. When we finish there, he tells me to go back to Meemaw while he takes a long walk outside to get a breath of fresh air. I know it's because he needs his smoke.

When I get settled in the room with Meemaw, we talk for a while, then I finish my homework when she dozes off for a few minutes. When she wakes up, I remember what Captain Ar says about talking to Meemaw about Jesus.

"Meemaw," I say.

"Yes, what is it?"

"Why have you been going to church?"

She gets a real strange look on her face. "Well, Captain Ar said it would be good for you."

"But how about you? Do you like it?"

"Yes, and I've been liking it the more we go."

"Have you thought about the little paper Captain Ar gave you a while back?"

"Yes, I have."

"You know I've asked Jesus to forgive my sins and to be my Savior."

"Yes," she says, and her eyes get watery.

"You really scared us all the last few days, Meemaw."

"I scared me too. I'm not sure where I'd have gone if I would have kicked the bucket."

"If you know you've done wrong and need Jesus, why don't you pray and ask him to save you now? Then you'll know you'll go to heaven someday. When I did that, God really changed the way I think about things, and I'm happier than I've ever been. I even like school."

"Well, I've certainly seen a big change in you."

"Then why don't you ask Jesus into your heart and start reading the Bible and do what it says."

"Tommi Jo."

Every nerve in my body jumps. I know that voice. I turn and look toward the doorway. I was so engrossed in what I was saying to Meemaw, I didn't hear the door open. Meemaw didn't either.

There stands my mom and a woman I don't know. But she looks so much like Mom, she has to be my aunt.

I have no idea how long they've been standing there.

"Mom!" I practically yell.

"Hello, you two," Mom says and points to the woman next to her. "Tommi Jo, this is your Aunt Alma."

I jump out of the chair, rush to Mom, and give her a big, fat hug. Me giving two big, fat hugs on the same day are unheard of. "What are you doing here?"

Aunt Alma grabs me and gives me a big hug too. "How are you, my dear? So, I finally get to meet my niece."

Mom says, "After your father called and told us what had happened to your grandmother, we decided to drive in to see her."

"It's good to see you, Nancy." Meemaw raises her arms toward Mom, and Mom rushes to her and gives her a big hug.

Aunt Alma also gives Meemaw a hug.

This is turning into a hug-a-thon.

"Mom," Aunt Alma says, "it's so good to see you. It's been a long time."

"Too long," Meemaw says, her eyes floating with tears. "It's too bad something like a heart attack has brought us all together. But I'm glad it did."

"We asked for a few days off from work," Aunt Alma says to Meemaw. "We plan to stay long enough to make sure you're back on your feet."

"And … Tommi Jo," Mom says to me, "I couldn't help but hear what you just said about you and God. I've been doing some serious thinking about God ever since you sent me that little church paper."

"I'm so glad," I say. "I just want you to know how Jesus changed me from the top to bottom and inside out. I'm happier than I've ever been in my whole life."

"I can see that," Mom says. "And I really, really want to hear some more."

"Nancy! What are you doing here?" Pop is standing in the doorway with a shocked look masking his face.

Mom and Aunt Alma turn toward him. "Well, Tom," Mom says, "I guess I can come visit my own mother if I want to."

"Hello, Tom," Aunt Alma says. "How are you?"

Pop joins us at the bedside. "I'm doing good, Alma. It's good to see you again. It's been a long time."

I study Pop's face and his words. Both seem very sincere.

Meemaw pushes up straighter in the bed. "If I would've known a heart attack would bring us all together, I would've had one a long time ago."

We all chuckle, then Mom says something I've been waiting to hear for years. "Tom, I've been doing a lot of thinking since your daughter, I mean our daughter, has been telling me about God. Maybe we all can sit down and have a nice talk about things. I've been doing a lot of thinking."

Pop smiles in a way I've never seen before. "Nancy, you know I've always been willing to work things out."

Pop's always been good at stretching the truth, but I wasn't about to open my big mouth at this special moment in my family's life. I just stood there thanking God for what I was hearing.

I think maybe God has more planned for all of us than I could have ever imagined.

The End

RUTH MCGINNIS

"The Queen of Billiards"
(1911–1974)

Ruth McGinnis was a real person who became the first female world champion pool player. She learned to shoot pool in her father's barber shop in Honesdale, Pennsylvania, where he had pool tables in a separate room for his patrons to use while they waited for their haircuts.

She started shooting pool when she was tall enough to reach the table and used a stool when she had to reach on to the center of the table. She became so good, she ran forty-seven balls off straight when she was ten. Her dad would give her a dollar every time she ran twenty or more balls off without missing.

Ruth became a famous pool player in an era when women were not welcomed in poolrooms. When she became an adult, she toured the world, playing against her male counterparts and almost always beating them. She championed a woman's right to not only shoot pool but to also play other "men's sports" as well.

"I get a big kick out of beating men because they always seem so anxious to show their superiority," Ruth said in 1940 at the peak of her career. "Most of them play as though it were a matter of life or death. If I played that way, I'd be a case for an institution in a few weeks."

Read more: https://www.smithsonianmag.com/history/ruth-mcginnis-queen-billiards

REVIEW QUESTIONS

CHAPTER ONE

How does Pockets feel about her parents being divorced and Mom not living with her, Meemaw, and Dad? (p. 3-4)
Why does Pockets have to disguise herself as a boy to shoot pool with her father in Joe's back room? (p. 6)
What conflict does Pockets have in her heart when she sees Runner at the poolroom? (p. 9)

THINK IT THROUGH
Why do you think Pockets does so poorly in school?

ENCOURAGING WORDS FOR YOU
"Cast your burden on the Lord, And He shall sustain you;
He shall never permit the righteous to be moved."
(Psalm 55:22)

How could this verse have helped Pockets?
How can it help you?

CHAPTER TWO

Although Pockets is very lonely, why doesn't she want to make friends? (p. 15)
What is Pockets' one goal in life? (p. 15)

Why is Pockets accepted as a member of the Thorns' gang even though she's a girl?(p. 18)

THINK IT THROUGH
Why does Pockets love to run with the gang?

ENCOURAGING WORDS FOR YOU
"The Lord is near to those who have a broken heart, and saves such as have a contrite spirit." (Psalm 34:18)

Could this verse have helped Pockets when she felt so lonely? Do you know that God wants to be your friend?

CHAPTER THREE

Is Pockets brave or scared when she rumbled with the Thorns? (p. 22)
Who is Pockets shocked to see at the police station? (p. 25)
Instead of being sent to reform school, where does Pockets have to go for three months? (p. 25)

THINK IT THROUGH
Why do you think Pockets' father disciplines her so lightly?

ENCOURAGING WORDS FOR YOU
"Whoever has no rule over his own spirit Is like a city broken down, without walls."
(Proverbs 25:28)

Does Pockets have "rule" over her own spirit?
Do you have a temper problem?

CHAPTER FOUR

What doesn't Captain Masters know about Pockets that's a big surprise? (p. 32)

Who wins the "silence battle" in Captain Masters's office? (p. 32)

Which student in Pockets' class is the only one who has ever even said hi to her? (p. 36)

THINK IT THROUGH
Why do you think Pockets isn't excited about her birthday at all?

ENCOURAGING WORDS FOR YOU
"A man who has friends must himself be friendly...."
(Proverbs 18:24)

How could this verse have helped Pockets with her friend problem?
Do you reach out to others to be their friend?

CHAPTER FIVE

How does Meemaw surprise Pockets at the birthday party? (p. 39-40)

What does Captain Ar do that causes Pockets to start respecting the woman? (p. 42-43)

What gift is Pockets' favorite? Why? (p. 42-43)

THINK IT THROUGH
Why is Pockets embarrassed while opening her gifts?

ENCOURAGING WORDS FOR YOU

"But lay up for yourselves treasures in heaven, where neither moth nor rust destroys and where thieves do not break in and steal. For where your treasure is, there your heart will be also." (Matthew 6:20-21)

Does Pockets realize that the gifts she received at her party will not last forever?
Do you realize that things like gifts won't last forever?

CHAPTER SIX

Why does Pockets think her mother sent the pet alligator as a birthday present? (p. 46)
How does Pockets feel about her mother? (p. 50-51)
How did Pockets first learn about Jesus? (p. 51-52)

THINK IT THROUGH

Why do you think Pockets says she doesn't have problems, just "issues?"

ENCOURAGING WORDS FOR YOU

"And above all things have fervent love for one another, for "love will cover a multitude of sins."
(1 Peter 4:8)

Does Pockets realize that loving someone involves forgiving them?
Has anyone hurt you whom you need to forgive?

CHAPTER SEVEN

Why is Pockets shocked at the news Leona tells her about Runner? (p. 57)
What interrupts Pockets' schedule to get the living room cleaned and make the pork chop supper? (p. 60)
Why did Pockets really love shooting pool with Pop at Joe's this particular time? (p. 62-63)

THINK IT THROUGH
Why does Pockets and her dad lose the match?

ENCOURAGING WORDS FOR YOU
"Come to Me, all you who labor and are heavy laden, and I will give you rest."
(Matthew 11:28)

Has Pockets ever realized that God can give her strength and rest when she works so hard?
Do you ever ask God to help you do hard jobs?

CHAPTER EIGHT

What does Mom say that breaks Pockets' heart? (p.67)
What does Pockets learn about Ruth McGinnis? (p.69-70)
Who is at the Friday Fun Night that totally surprises Pockets? (p.72)

THINK IT THROUGH
Why is Pockets so embarrassed at Friday Fun Night?

ENCOURAGING WORDS FOR YOU
"And now abide faith, hope, love, these three; but the greatest of these is love."
(1 Corinthians 13:13)

Is Pockets starting to feel love from Captain Ar and the other kids?
Do you show love to others even though they might not return the love?

CHAPTER NINE

What is the biggest surprise, by far, that Pockets learns about Captain Ar? (p.77)
What does Pockets come to realize about her disguising herself as a boy to shoot pool at Joe's? (p.83)
When Pockets drifts off to sleep, what is she thinking about? (p.86)

THINK IT THROUGH
What do you think helps Pockets have a good attitude about helping Meemaw and Pop with the corn project?

ENCOURAGING WORDS FOR YOU
"That if you confess with your mouth the Lord Jesus and believe in your heart that God has raised Him from the dead, you will be saved."
(Romans 10:9)

Is Pockets finally starting to understand the meaning of "being saved?"

Have you ever asked Jesus to come into your life and save you, so you can be with Him in heaven forever someday?

CHAPTER TEN

What kind of phone call has Pockets been waiting for all her life? (p.87)
How is Pockets' attitude changing about her counseling with Captain Ar? (p.88)
What does Pockets do in her counseling session that changes the entire direction of her life and future? (p.92)

THINK IT THROUGH
Why does Pockets consider backing out of her bowling date with the girls?

ENCOURAGING WORDS FOR YOU
"But God demonstrates His own love toward us, in that while we were still sinners, Christ died for us."
(Romans 5:8)

Does Pockets admit that her "mistakes" are really sins?
How about you?

CHAPTER ELEVEN

What does Pockets do at Friday Fun Night that surprises everyone? (p.95)
Who shows up at Joe's that thrills Pockets? (p.97)
What does Pockets do at the poolroom that completely disappoints her dad? (p.99)

THINK IT THROUGH
Why do you think Pockets takes her hat off so everyone will know she's a girl?

ENCOURAGING WORDS FOR YOU
"If we say that we have fellowship with Him, and walk in darkness, we lie and do not practice the truth."
(1 John 1:6)

Does Pockets realize that deception is a form of lying?
Have you ever tried to deceive anyone?

CHAPTER TWELVE

What does Pockets finally tell Meemaw and Pop when they are at Captain Ar's office? (p.105)
What does Pockets do to get ready for school that's completely different from anything she's ever done before? (p.107)
What does Leona tell Pockets that just about "knocks Pockets' socks off?" (p.111)

THINK IT THROUGH
Besides getting to shoot pool, what's a more important reason Pockets is overjoyed that Captain Ar has invited her to keep coming to Friday Fun Night?

ENCOURAGING WORDS FOR YOU
"Therefore, if anyone is in Christ, he is a new creation; old things have passed away; behold, all things have become new."
(2 Corinthians 5:17)

How is Pockets' life changing since she accepted Jesus as her Savior?
Have you accepted Jesus as your Savior? Has your life changed?

CHAPTER THIRTEEN

Why is Pockets so worried about her grandmother? (p.118)
When Pockets learns that Runner is competing in the billiard competition, how does she react? (p.118-119)
At this point in time, what's the most exciting moment for Pockets at the billiard competition? (p.123)

THINK' IT THROUGH
What does Ruth McGinnis say that makes Pockets more nervous than ever?

ENCOURAGING WORDS FOR YOU
"But He gives more grace. Therefore He says: "God resists the proud, but gives grace to the humble."
(James 4:6)

How does Pockets demonstrate humility at the billiard competition?
Do you brag about yourself or do you try to be humble about your accomplishments?

CHAPTER FOURTEEN

Why does Pockets lose the championship match to Runner? (p.127)

What does Pockets finally realize about all her "fame" and the trophy she won? (p.129)

What "disturbing" news does Pockets share with Captain Ar? (p.131)

THINK IT THROUGH
Why do you think Pockets is so emotionally torn about moving to Kansas with her mother?

ENCOURAGING WORDS FOR YOU
"For all that is in the world—the lust of the flesh, the lust of the eyes, and the pride of life—is not of the Father but is of the world."
(1 John 2:16)

Now does Pockets realize that "things" on this earth like her trophy will not last forever?
Do you realize that?

CHAPTER FIFTEEN

Who tells Pockets about Meemaw's heart attack? (p.133-134)

Why does Pockets believe she finally has some "friends?" (p.137-138)

Who comes to the hospital to see Meemaw and is a big surprise to Pockets? (p.146)

THINK IT THROUGH
Does Pockets decide to move to Kansas with her mother? Why or why not?

ENCOURAGING WORDS FOR YOU

"And we know that all things work together for good to those who love God, to those who are the called according to His purpose."
(Romans 8:28)

Does Pockets realize that loving others and sharing Jesus with them is the most important thing she can do in her life?
Have you ever told anyone about Jesus being your Savior?

ABOUT THE AUTHOR

Marsha Hubler is the author of the best-selling *Keystone Stables Series* and eleven other books. She's a homeschool consultant, an educator of children of all ages for over forty-eight years, and the director of the Montrose Christian Writers Conference. She grew up in Ashland, Pennsylvania, where her father taught her to shoot pool when she was tall enough to reach the table. She still enjoys a game now and then with her dad's pool table in her game room. Visit her at www. marshahublerauthor.com.

Made in USA - North Chelmsford, MA
1106357_9781951080068
05.14.2020 1117